Praise for *Positively Resilient*

"*Positively Resilient* is an easy-to-read guide to thriving in today's fast-paced, over-scheduled, hyper-connected world. The combination of science and practical wisdom make this book an essential reference to achieving resilience in the face of constant change."

—Mike Corkery, president and CEO, Deltek

"Why being your whole self—not just your "good" self—drives success and fulfillment: In our volatile, uncertain, unpredictable world, it is hard to imagine a more important quality to cultivate than the ability to be resilient. This book is an important, highly readable account of the insights and wisdom from the scientific community."

—Todd Kashdan, professor of psychology at George Mason University and author of *The Upside of Your Dark Side*

Positively Resilient

5 1/2 Secrets to Beat Stress, Overcome Obstacles, and Defeat Anxiety

By Doug Hensch

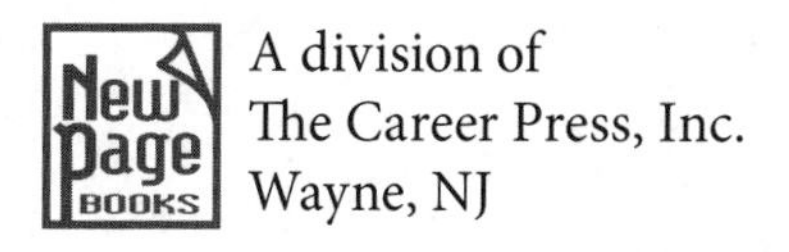

Positively Resilient
Typeset by Diana Ghazzawi
Cover Design by Jeff Piasky
Balloon image by Lightspring/shutterstock
Background imge by Iakov Kalinin/shutterstock
Printed in the U.S.A.

To order this title, please call toll-free 1-800-CAREER-1 (NJ and Canada: 201-848-0310) to order using VISA or MasterCard, or for further information on books from Career Press.

The Career Press, Inc.
12 Parish Drive
Wayne, NJ 07470
www.careerpress.com
www.newpagebooks.com

Library of Congress Cataloging-in-Publication Data

CIP Data Available Upon Request.

To Nick and Zach, the foundation of my resilience and
the motivation to learn and grow.

Contents

Preface

Do not judge me by my successes; judge me by how many times
I fell down and got back up again.

—Nelson Mandela

Several years ago, I spoke with a prominent author about my idea for this book about resilience. My secret plan was to self-publish the book and check it off of my bucket list. However, the author began our conversation by saying, "Whatever you do, don't self-publish…." She went on to talk about the benefits of having a publisher and I could feel my heart rate increase. The idea of pitching this to publishers scared me.

A short time later, I had coffee with two-time author (and one of the best coaches I know), Anne Loehr. Again, I told Anne about my idea for the book and that I was considering the self-publishing route. Anne also gave me several good reasons to find a publisher. In short, get a good publisher and you produce a higher quality book that can reach more people. My heart rate shot through the roof again.

What was going on? Why was I having this strong physiological reaction to finding a publisher? I spent some time meditating and came to the conclusion that my rationale for pursuing the self-publishing route was simply my way of avoiding rejection. Put another way, it was (in this case) a non-resilient way to address the situation. I realized that my (unrealistic) fear of failure (rejection from publishers) was driving me to possibly write an inferior book.

The lessons in that story are central to this book. Resilience is a foundational quality that can affect our behavior and our psychology in ways that we do not recognize. It is critical to any meaningful relationship and achievement. And you are already resilient. You may not react effectively in certain situations, but if you pause and think about it, you took the action of getting out of bed today, buying this book, and taking the time to read it. I would think it is safe to say that you have effectively handled some very difficult situations in your life. At the same time, we all have room for improvement. A nudge here and a nudge there can result in significant payback for us.

This book is *not* meant to be the definitive authority on the subject of resilience. There is so much more to be researched and written on the subject. I wrote this because I do not have all the answers and I wanted to share what I have learned from scientists, thought leaders, my executive coaching practice, my experience as a coach of various sports, and being a dad.

Finally, please do not read this with the purpose of alleviating the distress in your life. If you commit to learning and experimenting with some of what is offered on these pages, you just may be more effective in your pursuit of meaningful goals, which end up dragging you to higher levels of happiness and satisfaction with life.

1

The Case for Resilience

Expect adversity...expect more to conquer it.

—Marv Levy, former head coach of the Buffalo Bills

I have been writing this book for more than 46 years. Not literally, of course, but from a young age, I have been fascinated by people's behavior in difficult situations. I have seen my fair share of resilient behavior and examples of people acting not so resilient. I have witnessed this in my own behavior and thought patterns as well. I can vividly remember being 14 years old and screaming at my older sister to get out of the bathroom. (Sorry, Kath.) I also recall being engaged in so much negative thinking before a football game my senior year at the University of Pennsylvania that I threw two interceptions; held the ball too long, which allowed 10 sacks; and I was replaced at the end of the game. It was only our second contest of the year and I returned to the starting lineup the next week, but my season was over. My pessimistic thinking got in the way of several comebacks and ruined my performance. (Sorry, guys.)

Little did I know that a psychology professor was studying optimism and pessimism just a few blocks from our stadium. Dr. Martin Seligman is called the "Father of Positive Psychology" and he published *Learned Optimism: How to Change Your Mind and Your Life* during my senior year. Seligman's main thesis was two-fold. First, he argued that being optimistic led to better outcomes in sports, politics,

work, and school. The second pillar was that we could actually learn how to be more optimistic. Unfortunately, I didn't get a copy of the book and I continued to throw interceptions and my pessimistic thinking followed me through the entire season.[1]

It didn't end there, as my first job out of college was with a large payroll company as a salesman. Every day, from 9 a.m. to 5 p.m., I made cold calls in person and over the phone. On Tuesday mornings, we had what was referred to as a "phone blitz." Our managers gave us lists of companies to cold call and we were on the phones, non-stop, for three hours. It was brutal. People routinely hung up on me. They were rude and some even yelled at me, saying that if I ever called back…well, you get the point.

Every once in a while, I needed a break. If you took too many breaks, your manager would inquire about what was wrong and quietly escort you back to your desk while telling you, "It's a numbers game, Doug. You make more sales when you make more calls. Don't take it personally when you get rejected." Then I usually got some encouragement and ignored it completely. After about six months of doing this, I started to look for another job. I had no faith in my ability to sell payroll services and I wanted to quit. In fact, it started to affect my feelings of self-worth and overall confidence as a person.

So, now you understand that my default tendency is to be pessimistic when the going gets tough. I am also an "intravert" (I spell it with an "a" because it signals that I get my energy from within), and guess who I tend to seek out when I'm troubled? That's right, me. So, the spiraling down used to be pretty dramatic. I tell you this because being resilient is not so easy for me. I have been studying this concept for a long time and want to share what I have learned through the years with as many people as possible. In fact, I have spent the better part of the last 11 years finding new tools, tips, and methods for fighting through tough times and even thriving in them. Although I hesitate to refer to myself as an expert, I can tell you that I work at being more resilient every day. One day I might need to work on my flexibility while the next it is my optimistic thinking. Or, I could be spending so much time alone that I remember to re-engage in supportive relationships.

Learning about this did not happen overnight. It wasn't until almost 11 years ago that I realized there were psychologists studying happiness, engagement, meaning, purpose, and resilience using the scientific method. In 2005, a *Time* magazine article featuring the research of Martin Seligman, Ed Diener, Richard Davidson, and Robert Emmons focused on "positive psychology." They talked about happiness exercises and how they have been studying this for decades. Their research pointed to happiness and well-being as characteristics that were likely to lead to promotions at work, more satisfying relationships, less depression, and higher levels of achievement in school and sports.[2]

I read that edition of *Time* from cover to cover. I talked about it with everyone I could and bought several books on the subject. In short, I was hooked and (as my best friend would say) it almost became an obsession. For example, I started to practice gratitude when arriving home from work to help me transition from being a manager to being a husband and a dad. What I quickly realized, however, was that being happy and expressing gratitude only got you so far. It wasn't always enough to help me cope with life's ups and downs. And, this realization kick-started a more concerted effort to determine what makes some people resilient while others are less hardy and break down in the face of adversity.

Before exploring the concept of resilience, however, let's come up with a common definition. When we ask workshop participants to throw out words that come to mind when they hear the word "resilience," we routinely hear:

- Strong.
- Flexible.
- Agile.
- Bend but don't break.

This discussion goes on for several minutes and we almost never escape the exercise without also hearing the words "bounce back." In fact, Webster's Dictionary offers the following as one of the definitions: "The ability of something to return to its original shape after it has been pulled, stretched, pressed, bent, etc."[3] An article that I read about resilience on *Inc.* magazine's website defined it this way: "The capacity to recover quickly from difficulties; toughness."[4] When applying this definition to a psychological state of mind, we would say that resilient people are able to get back to "normal" after a divorce, being laid off from work, or even the death of a loved one. I do not disagree with this concept.

However, I offer up that resilience is much more than just bouncing back.

Bouncing back is critical but it does not tell the whole story. Bouncing back also implies that we return to our original shape. That is, we are supposed to be the same as we were before we were hit with adversity. My experience with resilient people is that they are never the same after effectively managing adversity. In some cases, resilient people experience a profound amount of growth and can be more empathic. And adversity can be linked to more psychological flexibility, more loving and caring behaviors, and can lead to more optimistic thinking.

When I consider the academic research and my own experiences combined with thousands of interactions with clients, friends, and family, it is easy for me to see that resilient people are not just capable of bouncing back in spite of adversity, they are stronger *because* of the adversities they faced and *how* they faced them.

Gwen Farley, an attorney for the state of New Jersey and mother of two teenagers, has been fighting to keep the environment safe for more than 10 years. When I asked Gwen if she was resilient, she quickly answered, "I am now! I really don't think I was before." For three years, Gwen helped her husband Marc fight a rare, deadly form of cancer that ended up claiming his life. She is adamant that her experience offered her no choice but to "stay strong" and "continue standing." Of course, her love for Marc was a driving force, but so was the meaning and purpose she derived from caring for two children. What I have come to understand about resilience is that it is a much deeper, richer, and more complex construct than just bouncing back. Although Gwen would do almost anything to have Marc back, there is no doubt that she is stronger today.

Growth is an essential element of resilience. Resilient people learn from the situations they confront as well as the mistakes they make. They are then capable of taking that knowledge and changing their approach as opposed to saying, "Well, there was nothing I could do better." Or, "It was inevitable." Resilient people are able to listen to feedback from the environment and other people while owning their own development as human beings. They seek to improve. Not that all of them love receiving negative feedback but, in time, they are able to process the information in a way that allows them to grow.

Because they learn from their experiences, resilient people do not shy away from difficulties. They do not shrink from a challenge. In fact, when challenges are presented, those with an abundance of resilience can be motivated by what is in front of them. Instead of contemplating how bad their situation is, what could go wrong, and the consequences of the worst possible outcomes, they can reframe the scenario into a challenge or a game to test their abilities.

Jennifer, a manager at a Fortune 100 company, is a single mother to two kids with severe disabilities. When things get tough for her, she recalls a scene from one of my favorite Disney movies, *Finding Nemo*, in which Dory tells Marlin to "just keep swimming…just keep swimming." Jennifer knows that after a first marriage to an alcoholic, dealing with several verbally abusive boyfriends, and raising two beautiful kids (now in their 20s), she just needs a little reminder from a children's movie.

Another element that we see in most resilient people is the belief in their abilities. They have the confidence and a sense of hope that they can handle the situation in front of them. They are not overly optimistic, however. They know that they usually have the resources (including the help of others) to come through okay.

Jim, an elementary school teacher who focuses on writing skills with his students, almost never backs down from a challenge. He is routinely subjected to what seem like interrogations from highly educated, affluent parents in his school district. His methods are questioned. Grades are a point of argument and recommendations for remedial work are often met with skepticism. He is often asked to give his credentials as part of the rationalization. Instead of making it a battle, Jim empathizes with the parents because Jim is a parent himself. And, he tells himself that he is the expert in the room. He is the one who is qualified to teach the child and make recommendations. Jim listens to the parents' recommendations and stands up for himself because of his years of experience in the classroom, his education, and his intuition.

Chang Liu (pronounced *Chung Leo*), director of library services in Loudoun County, Virginia, was born in China shortly after the Cultural Revolution led by Mao Zedong. When I listen to stories of Chang growing up in a one-room apartment and not having much in the way of material goods, it is not hard to think of how difficult life must have been under these conditions. She says it really wasn't that bad because "everyone in China was poor back then." Chang only tells me about this because I ask her specific questions. She is not burdened by her past, nor does she use it as an excuse when things do not go her way. Her face lights up when she talks about her family, and her life's narrative gets really interesting when she shares the story of an English teacher who voluntarily got up at 5 a.m. to tutor her. This anecdote brings us to the last fragment of the definition: support and connection with other human beings.

Chang, and virtually everyone else I spoke with regarding the topic of resilience, pointed to other people when we discussed the sources of their resilience. In Chang's case it was her mother and the teacher. In Gwen's case, it was the connection with her kids and her incredibly supportive friends and family. On the contrary, one of the most iconic figures in the last 50 years may be the cause of the biggest myth associated with resilience: the belief that resilience is a characteristic of the individual alone. The Marlboro Man (part of a cigarette ad developed in the 1950s) is a lone cowboy toughing it out in wilderness conditions. However, the research is clear that we really do need close, supportive, intimate relationships with other human beings to thrive and be resilient. (Later, we will also discuss how resilience can be shared with or stolen from others.)

Another iconic figure, Steve Jobs (founder and former CEO of Apple), has received many accolades for his technological and business prowess. He was instrumental in many areas of the computer revolution. His achievements are unquestionable: Apple computers, the iPhone, the iPod, the iPad, and iTunes, to name a few. He and Apple have truly changed the world, and not always for the better (we'll talk about technology and resilience later). And many times, his business, marketing, and technological accomplishments required overcoming many difficult obstacles. Apple faced bankruptcy, his new product ideas were up against timelines that seemed impossible, and technical glitches constantly stressed the team.

Many would say that Jobs was resilient because of these things. I disagree with this notion. Jobs was brilliant and he did demonstrate the ability to bounce back, but he could be incredibly cruel in the process. Some of his employees were able to thrive under the pressure of his leadership, yet others wilted as he threw out insults, denied financial rewards, and ridiculed their hard work. Some close to him said he had some narcissistic tendencies that made him incredibly self-centered; this self-centeredness probably lowered his capacity to empathize with others. Yes, Jobs was focused on his goals and helped many reach untold levels of wealth and success, but he left a number of people in his wake.

Jobs is often lauded for his ability to imagine, design, and produce unbelievable products. (I'm writing this book on a MacBook Air!) He was wary of market research because he was creating technology that people did not yet know they needed. Many times, Jobs just knew he was right...until he wasn't. For example, he hired John Scully to run Apple in the early 1980s. Scully later had Jobs fired and then tanked the company. Jobs originally said that only Apple could create apps for the iPhone. He later changed his mind after several months, but never admitted he was wrong. And, most importantly, when he was first diagnosed with cancer, he dismissed his doctors' recommendations and pursued changes in his diet and other homeopathic options. His doctors recommended surgery almost immediately. Jobs spent almost six months experimenting as the cancer grew. There are some who say he would be alive today if he had simply recognized that he might be wrong and that there were other ways to look at solving this problem.

This is not a moral judgment of Jobs (or anyone). We all tend to exhibit resilient behaviors and we make our fair share of mistakes. Karen Reivich and Andrew Shatte, in their book *The Resilience Factor*, write that "resilience is the ability to bounce back from setbacks, learn from failure, be motivated by challenges and believe in your own abilities to deal with the stress and difficulties in life."[5] My addition to this definition is that resilient people create and sustain supportive, intimate, mutually beneficial relationships with those around them. (Too often, Jobs got what he needed from others while their needs were ignored.)

So, why write about resilience? Why is it so important now? First, resilience is a required ability in the pursuit of meaningful goals. Being a great parent, business person, or athlete forces us to continue on in the face of adversity. The parent is faced with a teenager who is...well, a teenager. The manager is given an almost impossible deadline to achieve. And the athlete faces tougher competition as she climbs the ladder, as well as injuries and fatigue. Almost anything worth pursuing is not going to be easy. It is the journey that we end up cherishing just as much as reaching the goal.

Resilience is not only valued in the pursuit of goals; this is the second and possibly most important reason for writing this book. Based on my objective and subjective view of our society, there is an enormous amount of stress, anxiety, sadness, and anger that seems to engulf us. To make matters worse, much of this is self-inflicted. Our fast-paced society is only making this worse.

For the last 50 years, sociologist John Robinson of the University of Maryland has been studying how people use their time. Although many of us feel busier than ever, when we actually start to track the 1,440 minutes in each day, we find that we are actually working less. People are starting to exaggerate how much they work, as it is now a badge of honor.[6] So while we may be "at work" less, we are more connected. Work is on our minds, constantly.

Some studies show that when we are at work, we are switching tasks every three minutes on average.[7] The impact of this is enormous. We never feel like we're getting anything done, we are constantly being interrupted and restarting, and even though we make progress on a project after some deep thinking and using our wisdom and talents, the phone vibrates with the notification of a new email. We then read the email, make three decisions about how to handle a new obstacle, and then the phone rings or someone stops by our office. This cycle continues throughout the day, every day. And, once again, because we're always connected with work, we have almost no time to relax and be with ourselves or loved ones. In fact, research shows that too much multi-tasking decreases the ability to solve problems and think in a flexible, agile way.

On top of all this task-switching (sometimes referred to as "multi-tasking") is the constant threat of economic catastrophe. The Great Recession of a few years ago was certainly devastating. In 2008, almost a million families lost their homes, an 81 percent increase since the previous year. This number tripled in 2009 when three million lost their homes.[8] And it was all over the news, day and night. People were (and still are) traumatized by losing homes, getting laid off, and not seeing a pay raise for years. A friend of mine worked for a high-tech company in New Jersey for six years. He estimates that the company had more than two dozen rounds of layoffs. His wife stayed at home with the kids and his income was all the family had to rely on. The stress of producing for fear of being laid off led to chest pains, lack of sleep, getting sick more often, and simply being "on edge" with the family.

I have a theory that we have evolved a new human emotion: overwhelmed. (This just happens to be the title of a great book by Brigid Schulte that chronicles our state of affairs in much greater detail.) Never in history has so much information been delivered to human beings on a regular basis. What used to take days, weeks, or months to reach us is now delivered instantly to our phones. As a result, the average American adult checks their phone every 6.5 minutes. The average teenager sends about 100 texts a day and most (almost 80 percent) sleep with their phones. As it turns out, all this electronic face time may not be so good for us. Although we think we're keeping up with email, connecting with friends, and staying on top of our work and personal lives, it turns out that keeping up with everything might actually be keeping us down. Research shows that frequent multi-tasking with social media is associated with higher levels of depression and social anxiety.[9]

The engineers and marketing folks at Apple and Samsung promise us higher productivity, connectivity, and control. And, as much as I love my Samsung Note 3 (after two years, its capabilities still amaze me), I am not sure that it can follow through on any of those promises. Eckhart Tolle, author of *The Power of Now*, writes that "resistance is the mind."[10] When we don't give our minds a rest, we risk constant resistance. The phone has become an appendage that makes it much harder to rest the mind. Research by Daniel Gilbert and Matthew Killingsworth of Harvard University sheds even more light on the wandering mind. A study involving more than 2,000 volunteers reported that participants in the study were mind-wandering almost 47 percent of the time, which resulted in lower levels of happiness.[11] This is a fascinating statistic. Almost half of the time, people are not present. When we're not present, we not only experience less happiness but we miss some important stuff.

I was at Disneyworld in March 2002 when the person I was with excused herself to go to the bathroom. I started to take it all in. The Magic Kingdom is one of my favorite places and I decided to simply be present. I noticed the smell of popcorn, the warmth of the sun on my face, and the Disney architecture that makes you feel like you're in a movie. I was able to enjoy the moment. Then, I turned to look at Cinderella's Castle only to see a beautiful little girl on a bench while her mom was banging away on the keyboard of her Blackberry. The two did not talk about what to eat for their next snack, the beautiful weather, or the height of the castle. The moment for that mother was lost forever. Little did I know that Mr. Jobs would make these devices even more addictive in less than five years....

Enter Sherry Turkle, director of the MIT Initiative on Technology and Self. Turkle has been studying the impact of technology on human beings for more than 30 years. In her most recent book, *Reclaiming Conversation*, she writes about the "subjective side" of people's relationships with technology. She wanted to explore the following statement: "It's just easier to send a text." What she found was fairly disturbing. Among other things, she discovered that college students are showing a 40 percent drop in empathy in recent years, which she claims is a result of too much electronic communication and not enough face-to-face conversation. Turkle also explored the effect of "always on" devices, such as your smartphone, and found that they are having an adverse impact on romantic relationships, family connections, work, and education. She describes online dating as "friction free." If you are not interested in someone you meet online, you simply don't reply to him or her. Through many hours of interviews, she cites examples of parents focused on their phones at dinner time or taking pictures of the family and posting them on Facebook.[12] Finally, the mere presence of a phone or laptop can inhibit learning and conversation. How often is a phone sitting on the table when you meet a friend for lunch?

Another study published by the Pew Research Center in 2015 demonstrated several interesting findings:

- 31 percent of cell phone owners never turn their phones off.
- 45 percent said they rarely turn them off.
- 89 percent said that they used their phones during the most recent social gathering they attended.
- 76 percent of cell phone users between the ages of 18 and 29 use their phones in public for "no particular reason."[13]

We pull out our phones in line at Starbucks because we can't stand idle for five minutes without checking email, the weather, the news, or what our "friends" are doing on Facebook. As Turkle writes, we have lost the ability to be bored. Boredom is simply a signal to look within ourselves for something interesting. In one particular study, participants resorted to administering mild electric shocks to themselves instead of being left alone with their thoughts. Now, when I'm in line at Starbucks, I look around. I make eye contact with people or I strike up a conversation with the person behind me. When my kids say they are bored, I reply with, "That's great news!" to which they respond by rolling their eyes and walking away.

In short, we are exposed to massive amounts of information on a daily basis and we crave these "hits" of information like a drug addict craves a "hit" of his favorite drug. We are constantly reminded of things we need to get done at work and at home. In addition, we're spending more time on mobile devices thinking we're more connected to friends and family, yet the data says otherwise. As a result, I believe this can sap our resilience and make it harder to deal with the nicks and cuts that occur every day. At its worst, information overload makes everything look like an emergency. At best, it forces us to make dozens (if not hundreds) of decisions that drain our energy. Diverting your attention to a screen to see who "liked" a picture of an ice skating cat draws you away from your 10-year-old son, who craves your attention.

Current Trends

When I was a kid back in the 1970s and 80s, my parents bought me a subscription to *Sports Illustrated*. Several times a year, there would be an offer to buy posters. On the offer page, there were thumbnail pictures of Roger Staubach, Terry Bradshaw, and other well-known sports figures. Halfway down the page was a dotted line (this is where you were supposed to cut the page) and below that was a form where you filled in which posters you wanted, the total amount (yes, you had to calculate this yourself), and your mailing address. Just below the form was some text that read: "Please allow 8 to 12 weeks for delivery." Not "8 to 12 hours" and not "8 to 12 days." Can you imagine how people would react with that kind of message today? I wouldn't want to be the marketing manager who was on the hook for that product. Today, if we want a song or an app to entertain our kids in the car, it takes almost no effort and about 30 seconds to have the newest song from Adele or the latest version of Angry Birds.

Some other thoughts to consider: Forty years ago, almost two-thirds of kids walked to school. Today, that number is down to a paltry 10 percent. Why? Is it a shortage of resilience? Not really. Parents are afraid to let their kids walk to school for fear of being hit by a car or being abducted. (Too bad our parents didn't love us this much.) And, we're wealthier than ever. Even adjusting income since 1970, families are making more money. I would argue that, overall, we have more material wealth than any society in history at any point in time.

So what? This is progress, right? In *The Upside of Your Dark Side* by Todd Kashdan and Robert Biswas-Diener, it suggests that we have an "epidemic of comfort."[14] I couldn't agree more. Things are easier in many ways. And, when things are easier, we get upset at the smallest inconvenience. Our expectations of everything getting to us quickly and meeting our standards are virtually impossible. The new technologies that marketers want us to buy claim to make our lives easier, but is this really good for us? If we're with a group of friends and we're talking about a certain movie fact are we better off looking it up on our phones or talking about it? What do we gain from getting a product in 48 hours versus learning how to anticipate the arrival over several weeks then savoring the moment it comes in the mail? Today's engineers are hyper-focused on making our lives easier but are they considering the impact on society?

The other price that we pay for all this convenience is a much faster pace of living. Although we consistently use the Gross Domestic Product (GDP) as a measuring stick for the overall health of an economy and its society, this is not necessarily the best indicator of well-being. In fact, higher GDP, as you could imagine, is associated with faster living. Faster living, in turn, is related to things like more energy consumption. When we have more disposable income we tend to buy bigger refrigerators, bigger houses, more electronics, and bigger cars. All of these, of course, consume more energy. In addition, higher GDP may be ratcheting down our ability to engage in self-control. Societies with a faster pace of living are shown to have higher rates of death from coronary heart disease and higher smoking rates. They also have lower rates of achievement and they save less money.

The point of this research with regard to resilience is two-fold. First, we see that greater wealth does help us achieve more comfort, but it comes with a price. We end up having less self-control and maybe not taking care of ourselves as well as when we're climbing the economic ladder. The second point is that our expectations begin to exceed reality. Life's pace quickens but we expect things to get easier. Because we have more stuff and we're engaged in more activities, more can go wrong. It's inevitable, but our expectations don't seem to change and we are disappointed more often.

As I am writing this, we just experienced the largest single snowfall in Northern Virginia in 20 years. We were pounded with almost three feet of snow in just 24 hours. Schools were closed for a week. People couldn't get to work.

Yes, things were difficult but we didn't lose electricity. No one was going to starve or freeze to death. Yet, my neighbors were livid that our street took so long to be plowed. Once it was plowed, they complained about how long it took and that the plows did a terrible job. No one realized that our county didn't have the resources to deal with such a spectacular storm and that everyone (including those driving the plows!) was inconvenienced.

According to some psychologists, our emotions have evolved through time to help our species adapt to the environment and survive to create more little human beings. For instance, when we're embarrassed, it is a signal to us that we may have lost our standing with the group. This was incredibly dangerous to our ancestors. Being shunned from the group meant almost certain death. The group provided food and protection from dangerous animals and rival groups. On the other hand, happiness is a signal that we are safe. When we experience safety, we can relax and be less vigilant. But there is a price to pay. We are also less motivated. If we have what we want, why strive for more?

Every one of the resilient people who were interviewed for this book either came from humble beginnings and/or experienced a fair amount of adversity at one point in their lives to help them stay motivated to make things better. Our school teacher from New Jersey, Jim, experienced loss early in life when his parents split up. This was a financial hit for the family, as it is for most people who experience divorce, and Jim had to pay for just about anything he wanted, such as a car, gas for the car, clothes, and so on. Almost nothing was easy for him growing up, especially since he lived in a wealthy community and most of his friends wanted for little.

Chang's family barely had enough money for one new dress for her a year. Her mom didn't just buy her a dress, as that would cost too much. Chang's mother would buy the nicest cloth she could find and then sew it by hand, saving every little penny she could. Chang told me that when her mother would give her the dress, she felt like "the best dressed kid in the neighborhood." In the summer, her mother would take her for ice cream, once a week, but her mother never ate. She just sat and talked with her daughter. It was only later that Chang understood that her mother couldn't afford ice cream for both of them.

Jennifer had a great childhood and likes to recall how her father was "almost gushing about how fabulous" she was at everything. Unfortunately, Jennifer's mother passed away at an early age, but her dad was always there for her. After college, Jennifer met a nice guy, got married, and had two beautiful children. Nice story, right? It turns out that Jennifer's first husband was an abusive alcoholic and her kids have a rare genetic disorder called Pelizaeus-Merzbacher Disease (PMD). Her kids' bodies do not form something called myelin, a covering that protects nerves and assists in the transmission of nerve impulses. People with PMD have limited or no ability to walk. They may not be able to talk, as well. Most of those affected are boys, but Jennifer's son and daughter both inherited PMD. Jennifer left her first husband and raised her kids on her own until remarrying just a couple of years ago.

And then there is Marilyn Frazier of Massillon, Ohio. Marilyn is also a single mother who raised three kids after a divorce. As the divorce was being finalized, she took a secretarial job for the city of Massillon. Marilyn demanded good grades from her kids and told them that a good education was the one sure way to be financially independent and secure. If you didn't get a 3.0 grade point average in Marilyn's house, there were consequences. In the end, all three kids went to excellent universities and two of the three went on to earn graduate degrees. When the kids were in college and Marilyn's daily parenting responsibilities slowed down, she went back to college at a state university and earned her bachelor's degree in sociology. Just recently, she retired as the head of housing authority for the city of Massillon.

I am not suggesting that you invent some adversity to improve your resilience, of course. I am asking you to consider reframing that which life throws at you into learning experiences and opportunities for growth and achievement. Jennifer, Jim, Chung, Marilyn, and Gwen are all stronger *because* of what they faced, not in spite of what they faced.

Ran Zilca, author of *The Ride of Your Life,* decided to buy a motorcycle, get his license to drive it, and then take it across the United States. Along the way, he interviewed a handful of self-improvement gurus and psychologists to get their take on happiness and the meaning of life. Ran did his best to prepare for bad weather, being away from his family, and getting lost. But, it was still very hard. Rain made driving very dangerous and missing his family seemed to be the worst part of it. It was agonizing for him to miss his son's birthday and not be there to help while his wife dealt with issues regarding her business. In the end, however, he knew that taking the ride was an important journey for him and he (and his family) would benefit from what he learned. In fact, because it was hard, it was more meaningful than he had ever hoped it would be.[15]

I asked Jennifer what really tested her resilience. She paused and said that she handles the "big things" pretty well. Then she talked about how when the "easy stuff is hard," that's when she can break down, lose her temper, or need a moment alone. She has helped her son into his wheelchair countless times, but every once in a while it is a difficult task. It's times like this when she just stops and says, "Are you freaking kidding me?" *Just keep swimming...just keep swimming.....*

Another issue draining our resilience is the idea of balance. Companies are instituting polices to help employees with "work-life balance." These policies include working from home, flex hours, and company-funded gym memberships, to name a few. The problem is that today's employee is more fearful of losing his job than ever before and making time for the gym is not an option when he is doing the work of two or three people in today's downsized corporations. Working from home simply adds more hours to the work day without a commute. When the kids get home from school, it's even more stressful.

One well-known organization eschews the term "work-life balance." Instead, the employees at this successful organization talk about work-life *flexibility.* The employees are encouraged to be proactive with making arrangements that allow them to get their work done *and* fulfill their family obligations, make time for their hobbies *and* build a meaningful life outside the firm. It is not always easy and it is sometimes met with skepticism, but there are people at the highest levels of the organization who are making it work. One executive I know never misses a ski weekend as he literally takes conference calls from the ski lift. Another executive coaches three youth league baseball teams while running his multi-million dollar part of the business. It takes a lot of planning and coordination with his staff and his family, but he feels it's worth it.

What do these people know that we don't? Just ask Marilyn Frazier. As Marilyn began to tell her kids about the importance of education, she realized that to secure her own financial future, she needed to get her bachelor's degree as well. For one whole year, she worked a full-time job, took classes from a state university at a local campus, and managed the house all on her own. Then, the kids started to play sports and participate in other extracurricular activities. Marilyn had plenty of friends in the area but she knew that she had to do the majority of driving to make this work. So she put college off until her kids went off to college. She said it wasn't a difficult decision because Marilyn knew what was important to her. She understood and had prioritized her most coveted values. For her, helping her kids succeed was her number-one priority.

Ann-Marie Slaughter is currently the Bert G. Kerstetter University Professor Emerita of Politics and International Affairs at Princeton University. From 2009 to 2011 she served as Director of Policy Planning for the United States Department of State. She was the first woman to hold that position. After two years at her "dream job," she quit. It turns out that she could not find balance in her work and personal lives. The position at Princeton offered her more flexibility and allowed her to pay more attention to her family. She recently published a book entitled *Unfinished Business*, which is an attempt to argue for better day care funding so that more women can enter the workforce while their kids receive the care they deserve.[16] What I think is sometimes lost in discussions about Slaughter is the courage that she exhibited to make a difficult decision and leave a dream job. In short, she knew what was important to her (family) and she has not looked back.

In addition to our epidemic of comfort, technology that keeps us "always on," and taking on more than we can handle, there is one more thing contributing to our hectic lives: choice. Economic and technological progress has brought us an unprecedented amount of choice to our lives. And, according to Barry Schwartz, author of *The Paradox of Choice*, all this choice is making it harder for us to make decisions, which is actually sapping our resilience.[17]

Schwartz believes that most or all of us fall into one of two categories when we make an important choice. The first category is what he calls Maximizers. People in this group go to great lengths to make the best objective choice possible. The objective of a particular choice might be, for instance, the lowest price for the product they want. They tend to agonize over their decisions. The second category is called Satisficers. People in this group tend to make decisions very quickly because they set up parameters for the decisions that make it easier. Keep in mind that we are all Satisficers and Maximizers at times. But, for big decisions, we usually go one way or the other.

An example of how this might play out can be easily explained when we imagine two people buying a car. Our Maximizer might create accounts on several car-buying sites, spend an extraordinary amount of time researching the value of his trade-in, and he will reach out to dealerships within a two-hour drive. Our Satisficer might simply say I am going to call the three closest car dealers, ask for the best deal they can give, and just go with the lowest price. On average, Schwartz found that our Maximizer was much more likely to get the objectively better deal but (and here's the real interesting point) he will be *less* satisfied with the deal. It turns out that the Maximizer buys his car but continues to think about how if he had just talked to one more dealership he might have shaved off another $100 on the price. He may also second-guess the service plan, delivery options, and anything else that he felt could have sweetened the deal. The Satisficer, on the other hand picks up her car and values it for the handling, the new car smell, and is happy that she got a fair deal. She does not necessarily settle for mediocrity; once her criteria are met, she takes action. In this case, she pulls the trigger on buying the car.

Not only is our Satisficer happier with the deal on the new car, she is happier overall. Why would a decision-making tendency have this big of an impact on a person's well-being? My theory is that this is adding to our busy, cluttered lives. We're overwhelmed by our to-do lists and our schedules. Maximizing a decision can take time away from areas of our lives that bring us more value such as family, exercise, friends, and even our careers. But it is the mental burden of constantly trying to make the "perfect" choice that really comes into play. Brigid Schulte's research into why working mothers feel so overwhelmed even when their husbands volunteer to make dinner stems from a question their well-intentioned partners are inclined to ask: "What should we have?"[18] It turns out that actually making dinner is not really the hard part. But when you add the burden of coming up with a menu that everyone will like, figuring out if you have the right ingredients, determining how long it will take to cook, and then assessing if it's healthy is what drives up anxiety and stress. And, so it is with agonizing over a decision; it's just stressful.

The other element that maximizing seems to bring out in people is social comparison. The theory is that those who constantly compare themselves to those around them are never satisfied. When we determine our social worth and self-worth through comparison we set ourselves up for failure. On a planet of more than seven billion people, there is almost always going to be someone more athletic, smarter, and better looking than you. Those who engage in too much social comparison will feel bad about themselves when they can't afford the nice car that their neighbor just bought or they won't really be able to enjoy the beach house of their friend because they want one of their own. Social comparison is not just for Maximizers, but they are more likely to look for proof of their self-worth in others.

Barry Schwartz published *The Paradox of Choice* in 2006. Since then, we have witnessed the introduction and mass appeal of the smartphone, which has put almost infinite choices at our fingertips. Imagine for a second that one of your New Year's resolutions is to be more organized. You want to stop forgetting things and be more productive this upcoming year and beyond. So, you go to the app store on your phone and do a search for a "to-do list." It's overwhelming (there's that word again). There are hundreds of choices and only a couple of ways to distinguish good from bad on the surface. Or maybe you want to brush up on your management skills, so you head over to Amazon.com and type in "management" at the top of the page and get more than half a *million* choices. Good luck with that one....

In the chapters ahead, we'll talk about five and a half skills (not half a million) that you can address to cope with and thrive in today's overwhelming, stressful, and anxious world in which we are bombarded with information constantly. One thing I ask you to consider as you read on is that these are not *the* five secrets of resilience. These are simply five areas that I believe can have a great deal of positive impact on your life. I believe this based on the research of the last 40 years and based on my experiences both personally and professionally. The next section will prepare you for change and give you some tips on how to prepare for the journey.

Take It or Leave It

- Take it from an introverted, pessimistic-thinking author: If I can be more resilient, so can you. Be honest with yourself, ask for feedback, and make the effort.
- There are scientists who have been studying happiness, well-being, resilience, and other areas of "positive psychology" for more than 40 years. Don't take my word for it. Do some research and go back to being a student.
- Remember that the type of resilience we're talking about is a rich and deep concept that enables you to flourish. While bouncing back is a key part of the definition, resilient people are also good at learning from their mishaps and finding motivation in big and small adversities. They know how to make deep, intimate connections with other people.
- While some people may be naturally resilient, others learned how to believe in themselves, take on new challenges, and bounce back over time. The resilient people interviewed for this book all dealt with major adversity and challenges to strengthen their abilities.
- It's not easy being resilient in today's world of "always on" smartphones, economic uncertainty, and social comparison. Give yourself a break and recognize that you are already resilient and you can build this muscle with a little time and effort.
- Remember that progress and achievement are good, but they come with a cost. Our "epidemic of comfort" may just be making us less resilient. Consider how your expectations are affecting your reactions to life's little disappointments. And think about how making something easier may not always be what's best for you, your family, your kids, or your employees. Instead of scooping out pre-made cookies on an aluminum pan, make them from scratch.
- This new emotion of being overwhelmed is simply a sign to slow down and reconsider your priorities. Yes, making

more money, having your kids get good grades, making a travel sports team, and getting promoted are all important. What I ask you to consider, however, is that they are not all *equally* important. Sit down and map out your top five to 10 priorities. Only one item can be the most important.

- Think about some of the bigger choices that you have to make and consider the research of Barry Schwartz. Are you generally a Maximizer or a Satisficer? Remember the consequences of trying to make the "perfect" decision. It's exhausting and actually leads to lower levels of well-being and even lower levels of satisfaction with decisions (even though Maximizers make objectively better decisions).

2

Getting Ready for Change

You must be the change you wish to see in the world.

—Mahatma Gandhi

Why dedicate a whole chapter to getting ready for change? While the following chapters contain the content that probably drove you to read this book, this chapter might be the most important. We'll talk about your expectations. We'll discuss some best practices and we'll throw out a bunch of tips to help make you more successful no matter what your goals may be.

A quick review of the self-help books on Amazon reveals some interesting declarations. One book claims to have "the seven principles" necessary to thrive at home and work. (The same author promises "five hidden keys" to success, happiness, and change in a later book. Which book is right?) Another book reports that you can achieve happiness in just 14 days, while another says all you need is their 21-day challenge. Finally, one book offers 500 things that I can be happy about. It's like a never-ending, all-you-can-eat buffet of advice and tips that guarantees happiness, fulfillment, and achievement.

I call your attention to this for several reasons. I have bought and read many of these books, and if I had just invested that money from the last 10 years into my kids' college funds instead, I would be home free. There is some excellent advice, research, and wisdom out there, but I ask you to be wary of all of it (including what you're reading now). If something sounds too good to be true, it probably is. Happiness in 14 days? (Or was it 21?) Seriously, don't buy into that type of claim. While the authors of these books (in some cases) have some great credentials, their absolute claims are not a healthy way to approach self-improvement and change. Absolutes are usually a recipe for disappointment.

The next issue that I have with much of the self-improvement content on the market is the lack of context. My good friend Todd Kashdan (the same one who coauthored *The Upside of Your Dark Side* mentioned previously) likes to say, "Context matters." I write this quote on a piece of flip chart paper in *every* class that I facilitate, not just classes on resilience or well-being. I tell participants at the beginning of any class to be a little skeptical and push back. "In fact," I usually say, "please make a point of it to disagree with me." The idea is that I don't want you to take what is written here as Gospel or that every word applies to you and the context in which you find yourself. Practicing gratitude, for instance, has been shown in dozens of studies to promote happiness and even decrease symptoms of depression. Does this mean that you have to write in a gratitude journal every night? Absolutely not. Practicing gratitude (and other exercises recommended here and elsewhere) may not have the same effect for you as it does for others. There is nothing wrong with you. It could be timing. It could be your current situation or even your expectations. In the end, not all of the recommendations I put forth work for every person all the time.

The Art and Science of Learning

In 2010, Marco Moreno opened The Basics Gracie Jiu-Jitsu school in Leesburg, Virginia. I started training under Marco in January of 2015. I was quick to learn that Marco doesn't just teach the world's greatest martial art, he lives it. He is one of the best teachers I have ever been around and his passion for the Gracie style of jiu-jitsu (GJJ) is evident from the moment you meet him. He is constantly watching videos in order to learn new moves to teach his students. He is also fond of sending these videos out to the members of his school.

In one video, Rener Gracie is talking to a group of business people about what he calls Entrepreneur Jiu-Jitsu (EJJ) and how some of the basic principles of the martial art can help you be a more effective entrepreneur and a more resilient person. In a principle he refers to as "position," he talks about how "using the right move at the wrong time is really just the wrong move." There are literally hundreds of incredibly effective moves in jiu-jitsu that can help you defend yourself from just about any attack from a "bad guy." Knowing these techniques is not enough. Knowing the techniques *and* when to use them is critical.

So, here is another recommendation for getting the most out of this book: Make it your own. Many studies have people write down three good things that happened in their lives each night. For some, this quickly becomes boring and lacks value. If this feels like a burden to you, try practicing it once a week. Or, maybe you speak about your three good things with your partner or your family. I do this every night with my kids and it has become a welcome ritual at the end of the day.

As you read, challenge the information instead of blindly accepting it. Ask how this applies (or doesn't apply) to your life and your context. Ask how someone in a different place may have a completely different point of view. Consider thinking about when something presented here *is* true for you and when it is *not* true for you. Not only will you remember more of this but you will be more likely to apply it. And, you will be building your "flexibility muscle." As you will see, being able to view a situation from multiple angles can be one of your greatest assets when it comes to resilience.

Another quote I put up on the wall for the classes I teach is, "Be comfortably uncomfortable." I first heard this from John May, a partner at one of the largest and most prestigious consulting firms in the world. John was speaking to a group of new employees about the benefits of working at the firm and the great resources available for professional development. As he talked about how they could reinvent their personal brands, he didn't say it would be easy. In fact, he said the opposite: get ready for this to hurt a little. Any type of growth opportunity is going to involve being uncomfortable. If it's too easy, you're going to be bored and probably not grow. Decide how much of being uncomfortable you want to put up with. Just remember that too much comfort probably means you are not stretching yourself. Being too uncomfortable, however, may lead to a decision to stop trying a new way of doing things. This is up to you.

And this brings us to our next point when engaging in any type of personal development: expectations. This includes your expectations and what you perceive to be the expectations of those around you. Let's talk about others' expectations of you, first. I was teaching a class on how to navigate difficult conversations a short time ago. We were talking about the expectations we have for other people and how this can get in the way of healthy dialogue sometimes. One of the participants started to tell a story that I will never forget. Her nephew was a successful accountant in his mid-20s but he hated his job. And he confided in his aunt about how he wanted switch careers but he thought that his dad (also an accountant) would get upset. His dad expected him to be an accountant as it was one of the most stable professions. She coached him through it and helped him understand that it was *his* life and gave him some tips for speaking with his dad. In the end, he went to law school, has a thriving practice, and hasn't looked back.

Another story has not worked out so well, however. A good friend of mine owns a business that he purchased from his father. His dad started the business almost 50 years ago and put his blood, sweat, and tears into it. He created a thriving company that now employs more than 50 people and has generated tens of millions of dollars. My friend started to work at the company right after college and never talked about it in positive terms.

Fast forward 25 years and he was telling me about some of the difficulties he was facing. It occurred to me that running a business like this could be incredibly draining and the financial risk was enormous. If you absolutely love what you're doing, though, you are more likely to make it work and see the challenges as necessary to fulfilling some purpose. In fact, the challenges may motivate you. Instead, my friend's *lack* of love for the business was putting a strain on his marriage, his relationship with his kids, and his health. I asked him, "What are your thoughts on selling the company?"

His immediate response was very telling: "It would just kill my father. My dad loves this business more than he loves his own kids."

Okay, so there may be some exaggerating going on with my friend but let's imagine for a second that his dad really did love the business so much that it would create friction between the two if my friend decided to sell. Who has to live with the consequences? Who works more than 60 hours a week to keep the business running? This is easy for us to see but hard when we're in a similar position. My friend still has to interact with his dad but the point is still an important one to consider even when we engage in something like building our resilience. Do this for yourself on your terms. Be incredibly wary of the real or perceived expectations of others as your source of motivation to change.

The other point to consider with expectations has to do with where you set your expectations. Some research shows that when participants in studies set higher expectations, they achieve more. I just finished setting my goals for the year, both personally and professionally. As you could imagine, I increased the targets over what I achieved last year. I've been doing this for a number of years and have found it to be an energizing process that does, in fact, lead to higher achievement for me. When it comes to resilience, however, I ask that you reflect upon this research with a grain of salt. There is additional research (more on this later) from Gabriele Oettingen that suggests we inject a little negative thinking into our pursuits. [1] As you consider this journey of self-improvement, spend a little time thinking about the fact the journey will undoubtedly have some bumps in the road. And consider *lowering* your expectations for yourself. Set small, achievable goals that you can track on a daily or weekly basis. It may be as simple as grading yourself on a scale of 1 to 10 every day and writing in a journal for a couple of minutes. This can keep you motivated and focused on your goal.

Another thing that can help you with learning and change is simply talking to other people. That is, become a teacher while you are a student. Learning by teaching also has some degree of support in the scientific community. When we consume some content (for instance, this book), we will most likely forget 95 percent, or more. When we take some notes in the margins or pause to highlight a passage, we probably retain a little more. (At its worst, this last method of scribbling in a book makes it easier to go back and look for the things you found to be insightful and/or relevant to your situation.) Imagine now if you decided to explain what you had learned. Your brain, instead of just recalling the information, now has to organize the information in a thoughtful, interesting manner. All of this "work" strengthens the pathways to the information in your brain. Then, when you "present" the information to a friend or colleague, your brain can take it to another level. You might get questions about the content. You may be met with challenges or you may remember there was something else you wanted to share. All of this helps with retention and can increase motivation.

Take notes while reading, whether it is in the book or in a notebook. Then, find a way to share at least three things you learned with three people. I know this sounds like a lot of work but it's another way to maximize your investment in yourself. The more that you talk about this, the more likely you are to actually *do* something and see improvement. And, your retention of this material will skyrocket. You will be making new connections every time you share a tidbit, answer a question, and recall the content. Give it a try.

Speaking of writing, give that a try, too. It's not just good for your retention of the information. I am talking about the positive effects that it can have on your resilience and well-being. The science is very clear on this: Writing about your experiences and your emotions is good for you. So, although it is critical that you engage in the exercises that make the most sense for you and that you engage in these activities based on what you want for yourself (not someone else's wishes), I will give you a very strong *nudge* to give the writing exercises a try. And, you will find that most of the research-backed exercises require anywhere from five to 20 minutes of writing to experience the full benefit. Of course, read this book as you wish. Keep in mind, however, that the more actively you participate, the more likely you are to get the most out of it.

Another analogy that I share with participants in our workshops is one with a family dinner. Imagine for a second that you decide to order Chinese food to be delivered. You go around the room asking for everyone's order and you put chicken lo-mein on the list. Someone else orders pork steamed dumplings and someone else wants moo shu pork.

You do this until everyone has a say. If your family is anything like mine, you go for your favorite dish (usually the one that you ordered), as soon as it is delivered. You might try one or two of your less favorite entrees and you go back for seconds with your favorite. When it comes to the material in this book, I ask that you put much of what you see "on your plate," including a couple of things that you know won't work for you or that you don't really like at all. That is, step out of your comfort zone to maximize your chances for growth. In the immortal words of John May, "Be comfortably uncomfortable."

Let's go back to our discussion about expectations. We've learned that possibly lowering them (in some situations) and introducing a little negative thinking can aid in our growth. More specifically, I ask you to think about your timetable for growth. Is your goal to be just a little more resilient? For instance, you may snap at your kids or your colleagues when there is too much uncertainty. And if you are simply looking for a way to snap at them less or see things a little differently, with some of the research and recommendations presented here, you might see some positive change in a short time. If, however, you are looking at creating true transformation, and if you find yourself really stuck and need major changes to occur to create a more meaningful, productive, yet peaceful existence, this will take time. And this is where expectations can get the best of us.

Take the analogy of a body builder. People who lift weights to construct larger muscles know that it takes time to see the results. They may spend hours in the gym the first month only to feel a lot of sore muscles but no significant growth. And, so it is with transformation. As an executive coach, I rarely work with an individual for less than six months. Coaching is not an inexpensive service for a company to invest in, so we often get requests to coach someone for just three months or to sit with the person and review a psychological assessment or their 360 feedback report. It just doesn't work like that. True transformation just begins to blossom during the six months and many clients opt for another six months because they feel the momentum of the coaching engagement. And so it might be with you and your personal growth. Don't short-change your efforts by expecting too much in too little time or with too little effort.

Let's also get some myths out of the way. Take a look at the following statements (without reading ahead) and decide which ones are myths and which are based on research.

- Resilient people are really positive and upbeat almost all the time.
- Resilient people are known for being able to go it alone without the help of others.
- Resilient people are the ones who never give up.
- Resilient people take so much pride in what they do that they tend to be perfectionists.

In our workshop, I read each statement and ask the participants to raise their hands if they think the statement is based on research. In most cases, at least a few hands go up for each one. As you may have guessed, it's a trick. They are all based on myths and it is important to address these as we prepare for positive change and resiliency.

First, it may be that the resilient people you know are usually the hopeful, positive, optimistic ones. You would be right in thinking that these characteristics can contribute to resilience, but I list this as a myth because of the picture that it paints. I would be independently wealthy if I had a nickel for every time that I was a little down and someone said, "Well, you just have to think positive." We put too much emphasis on feeling good and being upbeat. In contrast to this myth, resilient people are emotionally agile. They know that different situations call for different emotions. They don't see this as a war between positive and negative. Before you look at resilient people as emotionless, it is important to know that they do have a positivity bias. They recognize that a generally positive or optimistic disposition is going to be more effective (and pleasurable!) in the long run, but they reserve the right to call upon the most effective emotion in the moment.

The second statement is more of a myth, again, because I believe that our society tends to put a little too much value on the strong individual who seems to achieve more and overcome more on his or her own. I would challenge you to think of any high-achieving individual and how that person achieved so much. This myth doesn't really have much to stand on.

A friend of mine used to run a consulting firm that worked with a lot of well-known high-tech companies from Silicon Valley. He was at a conference one year with an entrepreneur who came up with the idea for a technology that many of us use every day and turned it into a multimillion dollar enterprise. While on the elevator with this successful entrepreneur, my friend decided to ask a question: "You have turned what was just an idea into an incredibly successful company. So, what would you say is the main reason for all your success?" The entrepreneur didn't hesitate and responded with, "While I appreciate your kind words about me, there isn't a day that goes by that I don't recognize how fortunate I am to work with incredibly talented people. And, I'm talking about my colleagues, as well as family and friends." Everyone from Abraham Lincoln to Mahatma Gandhi to Oprah Winfrey and Eleanor Roosevelt was solidly connected to a host of people that facilitated their success and their resilience.

The next myth about never giving up is one of my favorites. The word "quitting" has a pretty negative connotation in our society, as well. Resilient people do tend to stick with things and effectively cope with obstacles to achieve their goals. Keep in mind that resilient people are excellent at seeing their world from a realistically optimistic perspective. This realism saves them from pursuing goals that are now either unattainable or not worth the cost of pursuing anymore. By being in the present moment and recognizing that the circumstances may have changed or the path to success ended up being too costly, they actually make the wise decision and quit. What we see on television and in the movies, however, is the person who continued on against the odds to achieve a goal. This is what I call a story, and although it is inspiring and we need people to persevere through difficult times, we also need examples of people who quit when the quitting was good.

Angela Duckworth, a psychologist at the University of Pennsylvania, turned her interest in achievement into a career. Duckworth's research points to two elements that seem to predict high rates of success: grit (the ability to sustain interest in and effort toward goals) and self-control (the voluntary regulation of emotions and behavior in the presence of distractions).[2] High levels of grit and self-control contribute to more achievement and this is a hallmark of resilient people. But keep in mind that you can have too much of just about anything. Imagine staying in an abusive relationship because you are the type of person who sees things through. Or think about if you had a really bad boss who demanded so much of you that it was negatively affecting your home life. Resilient people are excellent at achieving goals that are in line with their most cherished values and sticking with those that are achievable.

The last myth is one that many people identify correctly but it's still worth discussing. And, while most of us know this is a myth, we're too hard on ourselves. We expect too much; we expect perfection. When we expect perfection we consistently let ourselves down. Of course, we are inherently fallible. There is nothing wrong with believing in yourself, but expecting no mistakes and always achieving your best is just setting yourself up for disappointment. It's not realistic.

Another issue that Tal Ben-Shahar points out in his book *The Pursuit of Perfect* is that it's okay to fear failure, but it's not necessarily okay to have an *intense* fear of failure. Ben-Shahar writes, "Failure is an inescapable part of life and a critically important part of any successful life."[3] When you strive for perfection, you may tend to take fewer risks. And, as a self-proclaimed perfectionist earlier in his life, Ben-Shahar writes about how it consumed him and how his life was completely focused on achievement. He explains how he lost out on the joy of the journey. The really sad part of the story is that Ben-Shahar ended up winning the national squash championship in Israel and he felt no joy. He was so focused on winning that after achieving his goal, he immediately started to obsess over how he would defend his championship.

A couple of years ago, I found that something was missing in my life. My kids and I were healthy. My business, then in its third year, was really picking up and the work that I was doing was getting more interesting. My skills were improving and I seemed to have just about everything that I really wanted. After some long walks and time spent thinking about my situation, I realized that I still had some growth to do in working through my divorce. I reached out to a local therapist (we'll call him Steve) and went in for my first appointment. Upon sitting down in Steve's office, he asked me, "So, why are we here?" I proceeded to tell him that I was as satisfied with my life as I had ever been but I wasn't satisfied with my ability to manage through the divorce and be the best dad possible. I will never forget his response: "This is the best time to do this. Your mind is open to new ways of looking at your life and you're not in a state of desperation." Of course, seeking help when you most need it is a sign of resilience. However, waiting for a rainy day to buy an umbrella may not be the best strategy for staying dry. Many of the tips in this book were born from years of peer-reviewed research, but please do not use this in place of therapy. This book was written to supplement what you learn about living a healthy life from other sources, including a qualified mental health professional. And, it does not have the ability to ask you questions and comment on your situation.

Still, there is a benefit from working on yourself when things are relatively good and stable in your life. The old saying "an ounce of prevention is worth a pound of cure" could not be more applicable. Have you ever gone for a run after not going for some time? Your lungs burn. Your legs feel like cement and all your mind thinks about is when the torture will end. Ease yourself into this endeavor with some small goals. Walk before you run and take on just one or two new habits at a time. Sonja Lyubomirsky, author of *The How of Happiness*, and research psychologist at the University of California, Riverside, recommends engaging in between one and four new habits, but no more than that.[4] This is probably one of the reasons why so many New Year's resolutions fail. People put too much effort into the list of things they want to change (weight loss, more exercise, new job, repairing a relationship, starting a business, changing jobs, and so on) that they fail to prioritize. One by one, their resolutions fail. Again, take a little bit of time to prioritize what is important to you and focus on the areas that will have the most impact.

Sometimes, it's just one thing that makes a difference in your efforts. Another tip you may want to try is, at the end of each chapter, write down the *one* thing that had the most impact for you, was the most interesting, or seemed to hold the most promise for you. It's a little thing and it's just one thing per chapter. This is a way to get ahead of being overwhelmed by all the exercises, stories, and research in front of you. Again, it's by limiting choice that we can sometimes make better decisions.

There is a proverb in the business world that reads, "What gets measured gets managed." It is sometimes attributed to leadership guru Peter Drucker and sometimes to Scottish physicist William Thomson (Lord Kelvin). And, within businesses, it is usually applied to sales. Business leaders are constantly fiddling with commission structures to change behavior. One month, sales reps may make most of their commissions on how many units they sell. The next month they may get a special bonus from selling contracts that are longer than two years, for instance. In short, by simply examining an activity (in this case, selling), you change the activity by forcing attention to it. It can also mean that producing measurements about the activity gives you a handle on it, a way to improve it. If you start adding up your sales volume every month, it gives you a basis for saying "I'm not generating enough revenue, I need to do more selling."

Another way to look at this is think about being a scientist with your life. As stated earlier, not every science-backed resilience or happiness exercise works for everyone. There are many factors that contribute to how effective you might find a given recommendation. Try experimenting with ones that fit your life. A friend of mine, for instance, read about emotionally expressive writing (we'll cover this in the next chapter) and decided to tweak the approach. As a single father of a 10-year-old girl, he was often frustrated and sad about the fact that he did not get much time with his daughter. Instead of ruminating on his situation, he took to writing letters to her. In the letters he expressed his feelings and always ended with how much he loved her. He's not sure if he is ever going to share them with his daughter, but he claims this is one of the practices that has helped him get through some very difficult moments.

If you are looking for some motivation to change, try measuring something. When we want to lose weight, we might buy a FitBit and track steps, sleep, and calories burned. If you play golf and want to improve your score, you might track the number of putts each round. Improving your resilience is really no different. The following chapters will offer you many opportunities to try something new or to even try something that you heard about before but didn't give it your best effort. Or, it might be that you hear something old with a new slant to it.

Either way, I urge you to try tracking this new behavior or exercise. If meditation is the thing you want to try, consider tracking how many times you meditate a week or the number of minutes you meditate. If you opt for a gratitude exercise, it might be that you track the number of things you are grateful for each day or the times you feel a sense of appreciation. The bottom line is that when you make a commitment to track something, you are more mindful about actually doing it. (And, if you're writing a book, try committing to writing 500, 1,000, or 2,000 words a day. Before you know it, you have a completed book!)

Take It or Leave It

- Question everything. Don't take my word for it or anyone else's. Research is great and it deals with averages and statistics. You are unique. Let science guide you but not dictate how you live your life.
- Context matters. Take time to recognize where you find yourself in your life and pick and choose the advice that makes the most sense for you. Adapt what you learn for your context.
- Be comfortably uncomfortable. Change that is transformative is going to involve some hurt. Don't let that be a sign that it's not working. If you're not at least a little bit uncomfortable, you're probably not growing.
- Higher expectations lead to higher achievement, but when we're talking about resilience and how we may need some quick wins, try lowering your expectations. Make sure that you are living according to *your* expectations and not that of your parents, a boss, or even a mentor that you have chosen. It's your life and yours alone.
- Recognize that teaching is one of the best tools for learning. Summarize a chapter or the main points for your best friend, partner, or even your kids. Share what you learn and share what you think is important.
- Remember that resilient people experience "negative" emotions, just like everyone else. Resilient people may be good on their own but they are fantastic at creating and maintaining supportive, intimate relationships with others. They give up when their goals change, circumstances change, or when the cost of pursuing something outweighs the benefits. Finally, resilient people know when good enough is good enough; they do not tend to be perfectionists.
- Don't wait for it to rain to buy an umbrella. Continually find ways to build your resilience. And remember that working on yourself when you are in a good place might be the best time to engage in a self-improvement endeavor.

- The enemy of many New Year's resolutions is not the goals themselves but how many goals we choose to pursue at once. Try only one or two new things at a time. Once you master something or feel that it has become a habit, try something else.
- Track your progress. Get a notebook and create a spreadsheet or write it down on a whiteboard in your kitchen. Find a way to measure your progress and you will be more conscious of the commitment.

3

How Flexible Are You?

We don't see things the way they are. We see them the way we are.

—Talmud

One beautiful September morning not long ago, I received a call from my good friend and colleague Bill. Bill is also an executive coach and has been in business for himself for more than 15 years. He has successfully coached executives at some of the best-known companies and universities in the country. In fact, Bill is one of the rare people to attain the status of Master Certified Coach as per the International Coaching Federation, which requires more than 2,500 hours of coaching to achieve this rank. In short, Bill is really good at what he does and I respect his thoughts on all issues regarding coaching. Unfortunately, Bill was calling to tell me that a client he had referred to me for coaching had chosen someone else to be his coach. "Okay," I thought, "this happens. It's not always a good fit and it's not the first or last time that I lost a client to someone else." I was disappointed but not devastated. I don't like losing a sale and I also recognized that this was part of the life that I had chosen as an independent consultant.

Then, Bill said those words that people with a low set point for resilience dread (yes, me!): "Would you mind if I passed along some feedback from the client?" I said, "Of course," even though I knew it was going to be rough and I really didn't want to hear it. For the next couple of minutes, Bill told me how the client said that I came across as too arrogant and that I missed several opportunities to coach in the moment. I immediately began to defend myself being called "arrogant," as that might be the biggest insult you could lay upon me. I was angry and hurt. But as I reflected back on the conversation with the client, I understood how this impression could have been made. I was devastated.

The rest of the day was not very productive as I kept going back to my conversation with Bill. It hurt and I was beginning to think about how my entire business may be in jeopardy and that maybe I wasn't as good at this as I thought I was...and the downward spiral began. I questioned my ability as a coach. I doubted my ability to sell my services to top tier executives. I started to believe that my colleagues would never refer business to me again.

Then, around 3 p.m., my youngest son arrived home from school. He sat down to do his homework while I checked a couple of emails, still worried that my business was collapsing before my eyes. Sensing that something was wrong, he asked me if I was okay. Since I do my best to model the behaviors I think are healthy for my boys, I proceeded to tell him about my conversation with Bill, how bad I felt, and what I thought were some of the implications for all of this: *I'm not a great coach and I'll get less clients.*

With a confused look on his face he offered up the following: "Dad, that's crazy. You're great at what you do. Your clients pay for you to fly around the country and give talks. And when I saw you speak at the movie theater (he attended my talk on resilience to members of our business community back in 2013) everyone clapped really loud and they were laughing at your jokes. They thought you were awesome."

I was dumbfounded for several reasons. First, how could a fourth grader be so skilled as to know that I was sad? And second, he was right! The points he made were all accurate. My thoughts on the situation were excluding the hard facts. I was not considering years of results that led to a successful business with satisfied clients. I had fallen into the trap of rigid, negative thinking.

Resilient people experience guilt, embarrassment, anger, fear, and anxiety just like the rest of us. They don't feel, however, that they have to be upbeat and positive all of the time. They get knocked down, spend a little time on the ground, and get back up. When they get bad news, it hurts them just like it hurts the rest of us. And one of the key skills of resilient people is being able to engage in what I call flexible thinking. They challenge their thoughts to find new ways of looking at the situation. They check for accuracy, look for made-up stories, and avoid all-or-nothing thinking. In short, they're the opposite of close-minded.

Imagine for a second that you are playing a game of catch with your 3-year-old son in your driveway. The driveway has a slight decline out to the street and your son is standing toward the street while you are up hill. You estimate the number of bounces it will take to get the ball directly into his hands because, at 3 years old, he does not yet know how to adjust to the ball. On the next throw you accidentally put a little too much into your throw and the ball goes directly over your son's head. And what does a 3-year-old boy do when his ball goes in the street? He runs right after it. You yell to stop him but he is so focused on the ball that he keeps on running. To end this made-up nightmare on a more positive note, let's assume your son makes it safely back to the driveway.

As you continue to play catch, you might question yourself with thoughts like: "Why doesn't my son listen to me? I've told him a million times not to run in the street. What is wrong with my parenting that he doesn't respect me? And what was I thinking by not playing in the yard where it's safer, or switching sides with him to prevent the ball from going into the street?" This downward spiral starts a pessimistic mood, which leads to lower levels of energy, a fight with your spouse, giving up on harder tasks, and even snapping at your son (who has done nothing wrong).

Now, for a moment, consider the scenario we just reviewed with one small change. Imagine that your neighbor is walking his dog and watches as you bounce the ball too hard. It vaults clear over your son's head and he runs straight into the street. Like before, you yell for him to stay in the driveway and he continues with an innate desire to get the ball from the street and (like before) he returns safely. Your neighbor, seeing all of this, says to you, "What kind of father/mother are you? How could you let your son run into a dangerous street? How come your son has no respect for you? And, by the way, why didn't you switch places with him or play in the yard where it's safer?"

If you're anything like me, you immediately launch into an argument with your neighbor saying, "I'll tell you what kind of parent I am. I was up at 2 a.m. with him when he was afraid of the thunder. I stayed home from work today because he wasn't feeling well in the morning. And, when he was feeling better, I spent about two hours on my knees playing Legos with him! Then, he asked me if we could go outside and play catch. That's what kind of dad I am!" One of the differences between the two scenarios is the difference between being flexible in your thinking and locking yourself into being "right" and not questioning yourself.

Arguing with yourself is a tool that begins with first recognizing that your thoughts are lacking perspective. We instinctively debate with our neighbor who tells us we're rotten parents because we know he is wrong and we're confident that there is another way to see the situation. We instinctively accept our own thoughts as the truth without arguing. The first step in gaining flexibility in your thinking is to admit there may be more to the story.

In the corporate workshop on resilience that we facilitate, there is an anagrams exercise that really gets people thinking. (Anagrams are sets of letters that don't make any sense as they are presented to you. To solve the anagrams, you move the letters around until they form words.) We tell the participants that they are to solve a set of 10 anagrams on their own with no help from other participants. Each anagram is on the screen for only 15 seconds. Their job is simple: Take the mixed up letters and rearrange them until they make a word in English. The participants get to work and immediately start shifting in their seats. They look around to see how their colleagues are doing and then the nervous smiles and giggles come about. Some give up. Some write down the anagrams they see on the screen in hope of solving them later.

After all 10 anagrams have come and gone, we have a big debrief on the exercise in which we ask a couple of questions. First, we ask them to imagine that an electronic recording device is connected to their brain and it records every single word that they said to themselves during the activity. Many people have trouble answering this. Others say something like, "Boy, I'm stupid." Or they offer up, "I can't believe I'm the only one who isn't good at this. I'll just write so that no one notices how much I'm struggling." The next question that I ask is about the emotions that they experienced. Again, the typical answers are that they experience frustration, anxiety, and a little bit of anger toward me for having them do this in a class!

Then, I reveal that only two of the anagrams were solvable, which usually brings about some laughter. The purpose of the exercise is to create awareness so that people can start to listen to what they say to themselves when things are not going their way. If, after four anagrams, you start saying, "I'm just not smart enough to do this," it's a pretty good clue that you are going to give up and miss the two solvable anagrams toward the end of the activity. And these words that we use to describe ourselves and the situations are incredibly powerful. We take them, many times, as truth. We fail to question the validity of the things we say to ourselves.

Perspective and Objectivity

Being aware of the inflexible thinking of another person is usually pretty easy. We're not the ones focused on an important goal and we're not dealing with strong emotions. We're also looking at the situation from the outside. Put these things together and we're able to see the situation much more objectively. When we're talking to ourselves and feeling intense anxiety, anger, or disappointment, we don't consider our thinking. Metacognition is the ability to be aware of our own thoughts, and this is one of the elements of flexible thinking. The real key, however, is to look for signs that you are not being accurate with regard to your beliefs.

How often do you say "I *should* listen more to my team" or "I *have to* go to this meeting?" When we make statements using phrases like "should" and "have to," it shuts down the discussion. These words create a mandatory response in which you follow through with an activity even if you don't want to. What if your team is not great at offering ideas? What if you could send someone else to the meeting in your place to free up an hour? These last two questions are not a part of our internal dialogue, so we end up going through the motions like zombies in *The Walking Dead*.

Recently, I had set the expectation with a client that I would send a proposal that she could review on Monday morning. I committed to sending it no later than Sunday night. I had every intention of getting it done on Friday so that my weekend was work-free and I could focus on spending quality time with my kids. Friday was busier than expected and the proposal did not get finished. Sometime in the afternoon on Sunday, I started to feel the urge to work on the proposal right when my son asked me to play *Battleship*. I almost said to him, "Sorry, but I *have to* get some work done."

Consider what "have to" is communicating to my son and me. When we use this phrase we are expressing an obligation to do something and we relinquish our autonomy; we are saying that we are powerless to choose another path. This is not the message that I want to send to my son, nor is it what I really believe. Saying "I have to" over and over again creates a victim-like mindset in which we stop challenging the status quo and accept whatever comes our way. What I ended up saying to my son was, "I would really like to play *Battleship* with you and I think we can do that in about 30 minutes. I am going to do some work for a client and I would prefer not to do it late tonight when I'm tired." Again, occasionally using "I have to" or "I should" is accurate and appropriate. Using it as an excuse and as your *default* way of describing the situation robs you of your ability to choose a different path of action. It creates a victim mentality that focuses our attention on how the outside circumstances leave us powerless.

As an executive coach and dad, there are two other words that I hear way too often. These two words rob us of our ability to think in a more flexible manner: "always" and "never." One coaching client recently said the following about her boss to me: "Jan always doubts my side of the story." The question I then asked the client was, "Cindy, can you define *always*?" There was silence on the other end of the phone, as there often is when a client becomes aware of the inflexible language they are using. At this point Cindy and I looked for evidence of how her boss had valued her opinion on multiple occasions. We also talked about the ramifications of using "always" in this case. It simply wasn't accurate. And it put Cindy in a place where she engaged in ineffective behaviors when she was with her boss. It is very rare that permanent explanations are accurate, but they do set us up for hopelessness. It is an indication that nothing will change no matter how much hard work is done.

Another way that we put our flexibility at risk is liking other people. More specifically, liking someone too quickly can be an issue. In 2007, while making a pitch to a group of investors for our happiness company, I was introduced to a man we can refer to as Tim.

It was January but Tim had a perfect tan. I noticed he was wearing an expensive watch that perfectly complemented his expensive suit. Tim was tall, had a great smile, and told us that he ran a "global training business" for a Fortune 50 company. Although the meeting was intended to raise money for our venture and we thought of Tim as a potential investor, he said he was so impressed with our idea that he wanted to come work for us. Without my knowledge, our CEO hired Tim a couple of days later and gave him a very generous salary on the condition that he would raise at least $500,000 and bring in several hundred thousand in revenue through his connections in no less than six months. As we were strapped for cash and customers, this sounded like a pretty good deal to me.

When I met Tim at the office later in the week, I remembered our initial conversation and I was eager to pick his brain. At one point in the conversation about our strategy, I mentioned that we had a very interesting product that I believed consumers would pay for if we could just put a little more money into the marketing. Tim's response was puzzling to me. He said, "Doug, the problem with going after consumers is that if we're too successful, we won't have the customer service people to handle all the inquiries. I think we need to stick to selling our products to businesses." It turns out that Tim didn't know much about running an internet-based business and even less about how to quickly and inexpensively use technology to scale up customer service capacity.

I recounted the conversation to our CEO and he said that we should trust Tim with all his connections and experience. A couple of months later, Tim had not closed any business and the one potential investor meeting that he initiated didn't go so well. Not one person showed up. Tim was clearly embarrassed; he had let us all down. I had another conversation with our CEO who, again, pointed to Tom's great network and his experience. This went on for another six months before I was able to convince our CEO that Tim was adding no value and had to go. But our CEO was incredibly slow to show any flexibility because he liked Tim so much right from the beginning. Liking Tim caused our CEO to put blinders on and make excuses that cost us hundreds of thousands of dollars. And it caused us to waste almost a year on a hopeless strategy. Unfortunately, a year was more than our existing investors could bear and we had to close down the business.

One coaching client of mine, Betty, was having a hard time getting along with her manager. I sat in on a meeting with the two of them and got a firsthand look at how they interacted. At one point during the meeting, the manager said that she was fully committed to the process of coaching and thought it might be a good idea to set up weekly meetings with Betty to gauge her progress on the goals we had created for the coaching engagement. Because of the strong negative opinion that Betty had toward her manager, she saw this as micromanaging instead of an offer to help and be engaged. The manager was simply offering to be a part of the solution and investing in her employee's development. My client's opinion of her manager did not allow for this perspective.

What happened with my CEO and Betty? Actually, they were at opposite ends of the spectrum. The CEO liked Tim so much that he was only able to see information that verified his decision to hire Tim. Betty was only able to see information that corroborated her negative thoughts about her manager. Psychologists like to call this the "confirmation bias." This is where we exhibit a bias for information that agrees with our current point of view. When Tim's investor meeting yielded no results, our CEO only listened to Tim's excuses and ignored the facts. In Betty's case, she ignored the kind gestures by her manager, only remembering the instances in which the manager had given her negative feedback. The problem with this type of thinking is that a very strong opinion can lead us to ignore information that could help us make better decisions.

This is why people watch Fox News and MSNBC. As study after study shows, these networks prey on the confirmation bias to make our society polarized. Fox News has a tagline of "Fair and Balanced." It is anything but this trying to portray all sides of a given story. Multiple studies from non-partisan think tanks, such as Pew Research, offer evidence that Fox repeatedly takes a conservative point of view and even promotes the conservative agenda. MSNBC, on the other hand, may not have a false tagline but the effect is the same. Commentators are masked as reporting the news. The majority of time is spent confirming liberal agendas and points of view. How does this affect our flexibility? Just like Betty and the CEO, we watch these stations and vote for candidates who oppose our best interests, for instance. And these stations do such a great job of preying on us that they ignite anger that clouds our decision-making.

Betty, for example, would say the following about her manager: "She makes me feel inadequate," or, "She thinks that I don't care about my team." These two phrases are usually a sign of rigid thinking. When you say that your manager makes you feel a certain way, you are giving him power that he does not have. Although it is true that others can have a positive or negative impact on our feelings, stating that someone else *makes* you feel a certain emotion puts you in an inferior position. In many cases, this leads to giving up on seeing the other person from a different point of view. It usually leads to labeling the other person as "bad" or "inferior" and we discount honest gestures to improve the relationship.

The second phrase from above (*she thinks*) is a marker for inflexible thinking because it's making a pretty big assumption. I have yet to find a person who can read my mind. Those who know me well can probably gauge my mood as I walk in the room, but the reasons for being upset or happy are simply guesses. Beware of claiming to know what other people are thinking. There are two reasons for this: First, it's impossible. Second, when we state how another person thinks, we place an undue amount of emphasis on internal, permanent characteristics when explaining someone else's behavior. In short, we attribute their actions to a flawed personality. We say things like, "He's disorganized," when someone shows up late for a meeting and is missing a key document. We fail to recognize that he is doing the work of three people, his wife just left him with four kids, and it took him two hours to get to work because of traffic this morning. We say, "She is rude," when someone interrupts us three times in a team meeting. However, her interruptions may stem from the fact that someone told her that you were lobbying for her best projects, her manager interrupts others, and she has been told that if she doesn't get her point across, people will see her as weak. When we are late for a meeting, forget a document, and fail to let someone finish their sentence, we are very quick to explain how stressed we are at the moment. Labeling someone with a negative personality trait leaves us blind to her good ideas. It is a failure to recognize alternative reasons for someone's behavior and it makes it much more difficult to connect with this person or benefit from their wisdom.

Finally, many situations that require our attention have us saying, "Either I choose Option A or Option B." As Chip Heath and Dan Heath write in *Decisive*, when you frame a decision or a problem in this way, you severely limit your flexibility to think and act.[1] The "either/or" statement creates a binary choice that, in most instances, is false. Imagine a simple example. It's a Saturday afternoon and you have no pressing obligations. You ask yourself, "Should I read a book or go for a walk?" This question, of course, tries to create a dichotomy where none exists. You have an almost infinite choice of activities. Strong negative emotions are the fertile ground where the seeds of the "either/or" framework are planted.

When Enough Is Enough

Is there such a thing as too much psychological flexibility? There are at least two instances when this can indeed happen. First, if we are considering so many options that a decision gets delayed beyond what seems reasonable, it can be a signal that we're being indecisive. In some cases, we're trying too hard to make the perfect decision regarding our situation. Remember Barry Schwartz's research on Maximizers and Satisficers? Maximizers try to make the "perfect" decision and usually end up less satisfied when all is done.

The second instance in which we can have too much flexibility has to do with time. First responders, military leaders, and others in fields that require quick decisions tend to require less evaluation and more action. However, this can be a little deceiving. It is usually through hundreds (if not thousands) of hours of evaluation that instincts kick in for quick decisions. It is flexibility in the moment that can be the difference between life and death.

When it comes to the "right" amount of flexibility, it's a judgment call. It would be great if there was a formula to help us evaluate more options and teach us when to stick to your guns, but this comes with time, experience, and wisdom. Life is messy and we'll learn some more skills in the following chapters to build more optimism, peace of mind, positive emotions, and a support network.

We have identified some of the major markers that indicate our flexibility is at risk. The good news is that there are a number of strategies to effectively challenge your own thinking and expand your ability to think and act based on the circumstances. In all cases, of course, being conscious of the fact that "something isn't quite right" is the first step. And simply being aware of our thinking is, in fact, a strategy with a tremendous amount of power. When we have a nonjudgmental awareness of our thoughts, they cease to have power over us. We are free to act but not compelled to react to the circumstances. In order to bring these thoughts to our consciousness, it can be helpful to hit the proverbial "pause" button. The ability to pause is distinctly human. It's one of the major differences between human beings and the rest of the animal kingdom.

Several years ago, my sons were playfully wrestling in the family room. At one point, I turned to see if it was getting a little too rough. Right at that moment, my youngest threw a punch that landed squarely on the side of my other son's head. After making sure my oldest was okay, I asked my youngest to join me in the kitchen. With his shoulders slumped and a look of resignation on his face, he blurted out, "Dad, he made me do it! He started trying to hurt me...." I let him finish and I walked over to our hermit crab, pulled him out of the cage, and asked my son, "What does the crab do when someone puts their finger near him?" We both agreed that the crab immediately slinks back into his shell. I then explained to my son that the crab actually has no choice between stimulus and response; he has a brain the size of a comma on this page. "The difference between you and the crab," I said, "is that you get to choose how you act in just about any circumstance."

And so it is with you. The next time you feel compelled to act in a way that may be unproductive or you recognize that your thinking is not considering your options, try the following steps.

1. **Pause.** Simply stop what you are doing, whether that is thinking, talking, or behaving. Reflect on your state of mind and pay attention to the thoughts occurring in your mind. Do not judge them as good or bad. Just observe.
2. **Consider.** Now that you have slowed down your thinking, recognize that you have options for your next thought, your next word, or how you will act. Consider the fact that you have multiple ways to view the situation.
3. **Choose.** Unlike the hermit crab, you get to choose how you think and act. Based on your context, pick the view and/or behavior that best suits you.

This may seem like an oversimplified way to gain flexibility in your thinking, but that is the beauty of *Pause. Consider. Choose.* In all the years that I have been coaching and training some very educated adults, these three words are often seen as the favorite part of a workshop or coaching session.

Wear Multiple Hats

In the workplace, we say that someone wears multiple hats when she is working in several areas of expertise or doing the job of numerous people. Although this is usually seen as stressful to the point of draining her resilience, the analogy can serve us well when our thinking is at risk of being close-minded.

In the heat of the moment, we tend to consider just one point of view: ours. When we intentionally put on multiple hats, however, we force ourselves to take different points of view. This can be invaluable when we're in need of a different perspective and don't have the time to gather a group of intelligent colleagues for their observations.

Imagine for a second that you are asked to describe the house next door. If you are in the front yard, you might point out the color of the front door, the big bay window in the living room, and bushes lining the front walkway. If you then walked to the garage side of the house, you might describe the garage door big enough for two cars and the pointed view of the roof. As you move around the house, your description of the house changes. It's still the same house but the picture you paint is very different each time you move. To add this tool to your resilience toolkit, try the following steps.

1. **Pessimistic Hat.** Go ahead...that's right, just consider the worst-case scenario for a couple of minutes and write down your thoughts about what might happen. Don't inhibit your feelings or thoughts on the situation. Honor your negative thoughts. In fact, it might be helpful to just let yourself imagine the worst possible case happening. Honor your negative emotions as well. Finish by naming the emotions you are feeling in the moment.

2. **Detective Hat.** In the late 1960s, a television show called *Dragnet* featured a fictitious detective named Joe Friday. Joe would arrive at the scene of a crime to interview witnesses. When a witness would start adding his or her story about the suspect's possible motive or get too descriptive, Joe was quick to say, "Just the facts, ma'am, just the facts." As we mentioned earlier, words such as "always" and "never" are

usually not true. Stick to the facts. List only that which can be verified and not argued.

3. **Cowboy Hat.** Think back to a specific period of history, maybe the Old West, for example. Ask yourself what history can teach you. Have you been through something similar? What lessons can it teach you?
4. **Optimistic Hat.** The goal of this hat is to reverse the trend of negative emotions and inject a little positivity to get you thinking about possible solutions. Feel free to be a little goofy. Ask yourself what's good about this situation. How could this situation make me stronger?
5. **Green Hat.** It's time to plant the seeds of something that will take root. You have looked at the problem from several perspectives. List as many solutions to the problem as you can and don't filter the crazy ones. This is not easy and it really stretches your mind to start thinking about some unrealistic ways to address the situation. It becomes increasingly likely that you find your best answer or you combine two or more items on your list for something more practical.

Emotionally Expressive Journaling

Psychologist and researcher James Pennebaker has been studying the effects of writing for more than 30 years. His research indicates that writing about your emotions can improve your physical and mental health. This strategy works for several reasons: It reduces inhibition, as we can be predisposed to ruminating about how bad things are for us, and it can lead to new understandings about adversity. These new understandings can be about you as well. Writing brings structure to your thoughts, which allows you to follow an idea to the finish line. Finally, putting your thoughts on paper can lead to a sense of detachment and objectivity. Here are the instructions that Pennebaker offers to make this work for you: Throughout the next four days, I want you to write down your deepest emotions and thoughts about the most upsetting experience in your life. Really let go and explore your feelings and thoughts about it. In your writing, you might tie this experience to your childhood, your relationship with your parents, people you have loved or love now, or even your career. How is this experience related to who you would like to become, who you have been in the past, or who you are now?

Many people have not had a single traumatic experience, but all of us have had major conflicts or stressors in our lives; you can write about them as well. You can write about the same issue every day or a series of different issues. Whatever you choose to write about, however, it is critical that you really let go and explore your very deepest emotions and thoughts.

Listen Closely

A theme of flexibility is listening to the language we use when talking to others and when we're just talking to ourselves. How often are you unjustly putting pressure on yourself? How often are you making demands of yourself without even being aware of them? To help answer these questions, identify a phrase that you use regularly. Consider one of the following:

1. "I need to..."
2. "I have to..."
3. "I should..."

For one week, count the number of times you say the phrase (or phrases) out loud or to yourself.

Talk to Your Opposite

What's important to you? Family? Friends? A balanced life? Find someone in your network who may not be connected to their family, doesn't work hard to make friends, and values work above all else. You probably don't agree with this person on some major aspsects of your life. Focus on finding someone who thinks differently than you. For instance, if you are someone who tends to consider people's feelings when making a decision, reach out to someone who finds it more important to first consider facts and data while being objective.

Take a curious perspective when engaging him or her and do your best to suspend your judgment. Don't make this a debate. You've asked for a different perspective; just ask your questions and listen with an open mind.

Turn Your Stories into Facts

A coaching client of mine (we'll call her Barb), once said the following about her team: "They're all just waiting for me to fail." When we assume we know what someone is thinking or what is motivating another person, it's time to pause and recognize that we're telling a story. And the stories we tell ourselves are usually designed to justify our anger, embarrassment, or fear. They demonize someone else, make us the object of unruly behavior, or paint the entire situation as being miserable.

These stories are so damaging because they take a very firm point of view that puts someone else, ourselves, or the situation in a box. It's a box that we can't see many times, and one that exists right below our consciousness, and we accept them as facts. We feel good for a moment because we're labeling someone else as bad and we're the good guy. In the long run, however, stories prevent us from seeing different perspectives and choosing.

Try this: Put a rubber band on your wrist. Start paying attention to how you explain situations that do not meet your expectations. This could be how others treat you. It could be how management leads your company. When you identify a story, simply move the rubber band from one wrist to the other. The basic concept is to become more aware of the stories you tell that are not necessarily accurate. The awareness of our stories robs them of their power over us. When we become aware of our stories, we start to see there are multiple explanations that broaden our ability to think and act.

Sometimes, just generating other reasons for an adversity can dig us out of a hole. In particular, when we point the finger at ourselves for all the blame, there is a good chance that we're missing other causes. Several years ago, my son was playing recreation league basketball. In this league, the defender was not allowed to pressure the player with the ball until it crossed mid-court. My son took about two steps over mid-court and the defender stole the ball and made an easy layup. My son took the ball up the court again...only to have it stolen shortly after crossing mid-court. At this point, his head was hung low and he pleaded with the coach to have someone else bring the ball up. The coach encouraged him and he gave it another try. Unfortunately, it was stolen, again. At this point, my son fell to the floor and grasped his ankle as if it had been twisted.

Within a couple of minutes, the game was over and my first instinct was to comfort my son and tell him it was okay. I wanted him to know that there were tactics he could use to prevent the ball from being stolen, but I know that was probably not what he wanted to hear, so I didn't start the conversation.

A couple of hours later, I noticed he was playing with some toys and seemed to be in a much better mood. I decided to try an exercise from Martin Seligman's *The Optimistic Child* in which you generate multiple causes for misfortune or adversity. First, I asked Nick if he was willing to talk about the game. Next, I asked him why he thought the other player kept stealing the ball from him. His response was, "I'm not very good." I drew a circle on a blank piece of paper, wrote those words in the middle of circle, and told him this was how he was seeing the issue.

I then took out another piece of paper and drew another circle. This time, however, I asked him how many slices usually come with a pizza. We both agreed that most pizzas come with eight slices, so I drew a series of lines within the circle so that we had eight slices. I then wrote, "I'm not very good" in one of the slices. I asked him what else might have contributed to the ball being stolen because, in most instances, problems have multiple causes. He paused and then said, "I think I went to the right side of the court every time so the defender knew where I was going." "Exactly," I said, and then I wrote, "Went right every time," in another slice of the pizza. At this point, Nick caught on and mentioned that he could pass the ball before he got to mid-court and that he might be more effective if he learned to dribble with his left hand, too. And so it went until the pizza was full of reasons. I could see how empowered he felt and he asked me to go play some basketball to improve his skills.

The next time you find yourself blaming yourself for the entire problem or even putting all the blame on someone or something else, try generating multiple reasons for the issue. Another twist on this is to generate multiple solutions to a problem. Anne Loehr is an executive coach in the northern Virginia area who has clients from some of the world's best-known companies. Several years ago, before Anne was a coach, she was stuck. She was thinking about her next career move and couldn't figure out what to do. She reached out to her coach and asked him to give her some advice on the matter. He responded by asking her to identify 15 professions that might be interesting to her. She got 14 down on paper and nothing seemed to really fit. The coach urged her to consider just one more and he said, "What about being a coach?" Anne relied on her coach for support but had never considered actually being on the other side of the equation. All these years later, she has found her calling and is coaching executives all over the country. Anne stretched herself and results have been impressive to say the least.

Take It Or Leave It

- Learn how to argue with yourself. When anger, sadness, frustration, or another negative emotion has you in its grip, stop and argue with yourself. Try to identify the evidence for your current state. Look for alternatives and bring some objectivity to the situation
- Don't be a slave to your emotions with immediate reactions. Take more control with a simple, three-step process: 1) Pause: Just sit still for 10 to 15 seconds; 2) Consider: Come up with as many ways to react as you can think of in 30 to 60 seconds; 3) Choose: Select the best path forward.
- Pay attention to the times that you say, "I should...," "I need to...", or "I have to...." These phrases limit our ability to think of other options for action in our current situation.
- Be judicious with the words "always" and "never." They are rarely true and they create a false sense of certainty. Be more flexible by limiting their use and reflecting on accurate time frames.
- Consider how quickly you judge other people. Did you like your boss the minute you met her? Did you dislike your neighbor the first time you met in the driveway? Both of these may be clues that you have not considered the "whole" person and you may be missing out on other aspects of their personalities.
- Get your news from multiple sources. Challenge what you read and or hear; do not blindly accept it.
- Stop saying, "He thinks..." or "She thinks..." In almost every case we are guessing at what the other person thinks and what his or her motives are. This only fuels the fire for beliefs that are largely inaccurate.
- Be wary of "either/or" situations. It is rare that we only have two options in any situation. Challenge yourself to think of more alternatives. Write them down.

- Are you trying to make a perfect decision on a car, a house, a job, or something else of importance? Stop trying to be perfect and consider making a "good" decision to help you move forward.
- Review James Pennebaker's instructions for emotionally expressive writing. Commit to doing it for three to four days and 15 to 20 minutes per session.

4

High but Far

The dictionary is the only place that success comes before work.

—Vince Lombardi

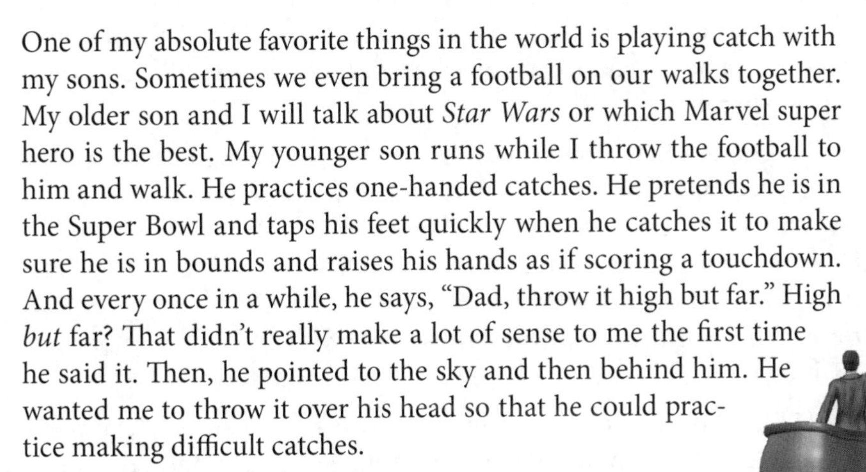

One of my absolute favorite things in the world is playing catch with my sons. Sometimes we even bring a football on our walks together. My older son and I will talk about *Star Wars* or which Marvel super hero is the best. My younger son runs while I throw the football to him and walk. He practices one-handed catches. He pretends he is in the Super Bowl and taps his feet quickly when he catches it to make sure he is in bounds and raises his hands as if scoring a touchdown. And every once in a while, he says, "Dad, throw it high but far." High *but* far? That didn't really make a lot of sense to me the first time he said it. Then, he pointed to the sky and then behind him. He wanted me to throw it over his head so that he could practice making difficult catches.

At first, he dropped a lot of the passes. As time went on after I threw him hundreds of balls, he got better. His skills improved so much that I couldn't believe I was throwing to a 10 year old. The point is that I could have praised him until I was blue in the face by telling him how great he was, but the key was practice and the self-realization that he truly was getting better. And we can't just wish ourselves or others to be more hopeful, positive, or optimistic. Some are predisposed to see the bright side or to automatically understand the good within the bad. Optimism, just like the other skills, can be learned.

Optimism is a very interesting and somewhat controversial topic. Much of what I believe to still be true was written more than 25 years ago by Martin Seligman and conveyed through one of his best-selling books, *Learned Optimism: How to Change Your Mind and Your Life.*[1] It is still one of the foundational books of positive psychology, but also misunderstood. Like much of the literature in this field, many have taken it to an extreme that the author did not intend. Seligman does such a wonderful job of painting a picture of success through optimistic thinking that it's hard to see otherwise. (More on that later.)

In recent years optimism has shouldered the blame for some of the difficulties we have faced in our society. For instance, in *Bright-Sided* by Barbara Ehrenreich talks about how wishful, positive thinking led to the financial collapse in 2008 and 2009. Unfortunately, much of the book references out-of-date, cherry-picked research and the author's motives can be questioned as she takes shots at scientists like Seligman to prove her points.[2]

Ehrenreich should not be dismissed entirely though. It is possible to have too much optimism and it probably is true that buyers, lenders, and Wall Street were too optimistic about the housing market. However, when I look at the research and the most successful people that I know, it is evident to me that the most resilient people are optimistic in their thinking. They are less likely to give up on important goals and more likely to bounce back when encountering obstacles.

First, let's discuss what optimism can help us achieve. Seligman's research points to a handful of significant benefits. He states that optimistic thinkers are:

- Physically healthier.
- Less likely to suffer from depression.
- More likely to do well in school.
- More productive at work.
- More likely to win in sports.[3]

The next question is: Why does optimistic thinking carry such a benefit in multiple domains? In short, optimistic thinking helps us see the benefits of pursuing worthwhile goals in a realistic (yet hopeful) manner and provides the psychological means to keep working toward these goals without giving up in the face of obstacles. The optimistic thinker, for instance, upon recovering from a heart attack, will take his medication, start an exercise regimen, eat healthier foods, and stop smoking. The pessimistic thinker, on the other hand, doubts the medication will help, feels it's too late in the game to exercise, doesn't see the benefit to eating healthier, and says the smoking habit keeps him calm. The pessimistic thinker may be saying, "Hey, my father died from a heart attack. My uncle died from a heart attack. It just runs in the family. What's the point in doing all this stuff if it is inevitable for me, too?" There is a sense of helplessness with this person and, just as importantly, a disregard of the evidence for trying harder.

The optimistic thinker tends to avoid rumination when she is laid off from a high-paying job and she is the sole source of income for the family. She experiences sadness when she is disappointed but the sadness does not dominate her life. Why? She is quick to focus on what she can control and more likely to act. The pessimistic thinker experiences the same sadness. But, this sadness becomes a long-term companion as she ruminates over how bad things are. She is slower and less likely to act on her own behalf to make things better.

Optimism as a Foundational Quality

In school, the optimistic thinker focuses on studying harder after receiving a lower-than-expected grade while the pessimistic thinker can't stop thinking about the difficulty of the course content. In sports, the optimistic athletes try to fix what goes wrong when they lose while the pessimistic athletes continually question their abilities. After being told "no" 50 times by 50 prospective clients, the optimistic salesperson says, "I have to believe that someone in the next 50 calls is going to say *yes*!" The pessimistic salesperson finds reasons beyond her control, such as the economy or the market for her products, as rationale to give up.

Dan Porter, children's book author and guru in the corporate leadership development space, says, "Optimism is the foundation of resilience for me." Dan goes on to say, "...for me it goes to the notion that a person must have a deep-seated belief in the ultimate positive outcome of this life's journey. Having a deeply rooted faith in the purpose of this life helps create both optimism and resilience."[4]

A simplistic way to talk about optimism is that you have it or you don't. In actuality, optimism has two major components that can be considered. First, it exists on a continuum. On one end is the Pollyanna-type thinking in which nothing can go wrong, everything always works out, and there is no time for worry. (This is the type of thinking that Barbara Ehrenreich unfairly accuses those in the field of positive psychology of promoting.) On the other end is nothing but doom and gloom. The universe is against the eternal pessimistic thinker and there is no light at the end of the tunnel. In between, there is nuance. There are slight changes over time and between people.

The second major element is context. In my experiences as a coach, I have seen major differences within an individual between work and personal lives. Some will say they are much more optimistic about their abilities at work versus their lives at home. Others are just the opposite. And there may be some subtle differences with regard to optimism across genders. Some studies show men to be more optimistic with regard to economic issues and the impact of technology. Women, on the other hand, tend to be more optimistic when they experience issues in their relationships.

In 1991, my good friend Joe Valerio realized his dream when he was selected by the Kansas City Chiefs in the second round of the college draft. Joe played football at the University of Pennsylvania. Since the 1950s, however, teams in the Ivy League have abandoned scholarships and it is only the occasional player who enjoys a career in the NFL. From the moment I met Joe outside of our freshman dorm in 1987, I could tell he was different. He absolutely loved the game and had a tremendous amount of confidence in his ability as a football player. Joe was (and still is) a very humble person, but when we would talk about our futures, he was never shy about sharing his desire to play football professionally. He fantasized about being a Philadelphia Eagle down to excruciating detail when he was a kid. (In fact, he used the swing set in his backyard to serve as the train he rode with his teammates up to East Rutherford, New Jersey, to play the Giants!) Many people doubted him, but the comments never stuck to him. He was Teflon to any negativity in this domain.

When his professional football career was over, Joe had no problem finding work in the insurance industry. I will never forget a conversation I had with Joe after he got his first job after five years in the NFL. He seemed a little down. He wasn't sure if he was doing well and this bothered him. Joe talked about how NFL coaches gave constant feedback, how practices were filmed, and every play was graded. It was much easier, he said, to understand what wasn't working and then fix it. In the business world, though, Joe knew he could succeed but I could hear that he was lacking the same certainty that he had displayed in earlier years. Through time, Joe has exhibited a work ethic and investment in relationships that has made him successful in this line of work. He may have had different levels of optimism in these very different domains, but he believed in his ability to improve. He took that confidence from one domain and sprinkled it in another.

What Is Optimism?

For us to have a healthy discussion about optimism, it is important to settle on a common definition. The one that I would like to offer up is: *The skill of focusing on the positive, without denying the negative, and channeling one's energy toward what is controllable.* The first dimension of the definition is the recognition that this is a skill, not just something you inherit. When I discuss this in our workshops, I do everything in my power when talking about individuals to refer to them as optimistic or pessimistic *thinkers*. The reason I do this is because we have control over the style of thinking in which we engage. In short, this is a skill that can be learned. The next part is what most people remember about optimism, but it is also the area that generates the most misinformation: *focusing on the positive*. Many believe that "positive thinking" is the way to optimism and resilience. Those who believe this are missing or ignoring the next part: *without denying the negative*. When I talk about how optimism can benefit an individual, I often say it is a "realistic" or "flexible" optimism that adds the most value. Finally, when we focus on what is *controllable* we are more likely to be successful. The unrealistic optimistic thinker may buy into the crazy notion made popular in *The Secret* by Rhonda Byrne that the "Law of Attraction" governs the universe. In the book, Byrne argues that when we think negatively, we attract negative outcomes. Conversely, when we think about good things happening (for example, getting promoted, finding a mate, and so on), the universe draws these good things upon us.[5] Some people swear upon this concept even though there is no way to test it scientifically. And when they don't attract good results they make up some reason as to why the Law was not invoked. The realistic optimistic thinker invokes the serenity prayer: "God, give me the serenity to accept the things I cannot change, the courage to change the things I can, and the wisdom to know the difference."

In *Learned Optimism*, Seligman talks about the markers found in our language that can give us a clue to someone's thinking. Making permanent, pervasive, and personal statements about ourselves is usually a sign that we're not thinking clearly.[6] For instance, if I say to myself "I'm stupid," what I am really saying is:

1. Stupid is a *permanent* explanation for my situation. I cannot learn anything else with regard to this and it is not going to change.
2. Being stupid is *pervasive* across multiple domains in my life. I am just not an intelligent person and I'm not equipped to handle life's difficulties.
3. This is all about me. No one else has any role in how things have gone wrong. I am *personally* entirely responsible for this situation.

Of course, there are situations in which it's not going to change, it's affecting all areas of your life, and it is actually your fault. I think it's safe to argue, however, this is not the norm and that if your default *style* of explaining events sounds like what we just reviewed, it's time to challenge yourself.

And this is where a little flexibility and agility can be an asset. The optimistic thinker does her best to consider how a particular adversity will not last forever. She also recognizes that most adversities do not bleed into all areas of her life. A mistake at work does not mean she is a terrible mother. And she is slow to take 100 percent of the blame for what went wrong because she knows that others may have played a role. It is not that she blames others but that she shares the blame in a way that is more accurate.

Consider Jennifer, the mother of two kids with severe disabilities. When she hits the wall and something goes wrong, she is quick to look at the situation with an optimistic view that allows her to not only recover but be productive and solve the problem. Jennifer likes to say to herself, "This will pass." She's been through so much that she knows difficult times will eventually end.

Steve, a wealth manager in the New York metro area, has been helping his clients achieve their financial goals for 25 years. In that time, we have experienced three recessions (one of them was the worst the world has seen since the Great Depression of the 1930s). When the markets drop suddenly, Steve must demonstrate resilience and optimism to his clients who are watching "experts" on TV talk about how bad things are and how bad they could be in the future. The clients see statistics and graphics that depict losses and no hope. Steve knows these dips in the market are temporary. He knows that his clients would "ruin themselves if they pulled out of the market" so he cites evidence of how the markets bounce back. Steve sticks to his convictions and focuses on the long-term goals of growth through sound investment while ignoring the short-term pain.

The Case for Self-Efficacy

One day a couple of years ago, I was driving to the store when my younger son suddenly blurted out from the back seat, "Hey, Dad! That's the school where I played soccer." This immediately brought some painful memories to mind as this was the spring that my wife and I were legally separated and the business I was running was close to shutting down. As it turns out, watching my son attempt to play soccer may have been more painful. He wasn't very good.

I acknowledged his comment and he went on confidently, "You know, Dad, I was really good."

More memories flashed before me. He didn't like going to soccer. He never finished one practice; he would run over and sit on his mom's lap before it was over. And, when the coaches lined the kids up for some drills, he tripped over the ball or missed the ball completely. In short, the season was a disaster. He was too young to be playing (4 years old) and he had no real interest in the sport or what it took to get better.

I was intrigued by his comment about how good he was at soccer, so I decided to probe into the seemingly optimistic little mind and asked, "Oh really? What makes you say that?"

Without hesitation he replied with, "I got a medal."

Carol Dweck, PhD, professor of psychology at Stanford University, and author of *Mindset: The New Psychology of Success*, would probably gag after hearing that. Dweck has spent more than 30 years studying the mindsets that people use to know themselves and direct their behavior. What she found was eye opening. In short, through numerous studies, Dweck found that most people fall into one of two mindsets: fixed or growth. Those with a fixed mindset tend to think that their abilities are inherited and immutable. Those with a growth mindset believe that their abilities, such as intelligence and creativity, can be developed through time from practice and learning.[7]

This, of course, can have a significant impact on one's optimism and resilience. (In fact, this theory may be the very foundation of this book.) Where this gets even more interesting (and relevant to my son's comment about the medal) is how these mindsets may come about. It turns out that the way we praise children may have everything to do with it. According to Dweck, praising children for accomplishment alone or for their seemingly stable traits produces the fixed mindset. This in turn leaves the child with no choice but to preserve the theory about their abilities. When offered more difficult challenges, those with the fixed mindset are more likely to pass on the offer, thinking that it may expose a level of competence that is missing. It actually reduces persistence in the face of greater challenge and obstacles.

The growth mindset can be developed by praising for effort *and* achievement. In turn, students with the growth mindset see higher levels of difficulty as a way to test themselves and learn where they can improve. Praising kids for effort offers them a template to follow, while praising a child for her ability offers no information on how to modify their behavior the next time around. It only serves to motivate the child to protect a set of beliefs.

The medal that my son was given was offered with all the right intentions. The leaders of this soccer league wanted the kids to feel that they were special and to have positive memories about their time playing the sport. Carol Ryff, PhD, a psychologist at Pennsylvania State University, argues that we are putting too much emphasis on short-term happiness and positive moods.[8] We are thinking too much about an individual's self-esteem instead of self-actualization and self-efficacy.

The impact on all of this in the workplace can be seen in the incentive structures of most for-profit companies. Bonuses and raises are given to those who sell the most or receive the highest annual rating. It is hard to argue with this approach as companies need profits to stay in business. The problem is that this focus on achievement can create a fixed mindset culture in which all that matters is reaching a specific goal. Employees start to miss out on the journey. They hear executives talk about "going the extra mile" for customers, but if it is not attached to a bonus, the existing customer is ignored as the sales rep focuses on selling new products that add revenue toward his yearly goal. All of this focus on achievement can even lead to a culture in which reaching the goal is all that matters and ethics are not considered. All that matters is avoiding failure. There is no reason why hard work and growth should not be rewarded.

Businesses that adopt a growth mindset create a culture of learning, feedback, and intelligent risk-taking. They value experiments and continuous growth. Companies with a growth mindset recognize that developing internal talent is a top priority. They may look outside on occasion to fill key roles but they look within first to send the message that growth is possible. Coaching, training, leadership development programs, and tuition reimbursement are the norm in these cultures.

Remember Chang from Chapter 1? She is the director of library services in Loudoun County, Virginia, and is a leader who has created this kind of organization. Not surprisingly, she values growth and education. She believes that employees can get better in their roles. Chang provides training for her team and sits on the edge of her chair in class, ready to ask questions and encourage her team. Remember it was her grade-school English teacher back in China who helped Chang understand that she could attend university. The two of them would meet at 5 a.m. every day to practice English. Slowly but surely, Chang's English improved and so did something else–her self-efficacy. When we discuss optimism it is also important to discuss self-efficacy. In fact, the type of optimism I am promoting is tightly linked to self-efficacy. Albert Bandura, one of the first to study the concept, offered this definition: "People's judgments of their capabilities to organize and execute courses of action required to attain designated types of performances."[9] In other words, people with a high level of self-efficacy believe they have the capabilities to accomplish a task. In Chang's case, seeing the improvement in her ability to speak English led her to believe in her abilities overall. This in turn propelled her to higher academic achievement and a spot in China's most prestigious university years later.

In another surprising twist, it turns out the optimism may not be the product of positive affirmations. That is, telling ourselves "I can do it!" may not be the best way to keep motivation high to solve problems. In one study, two groups of participants were formed and instructed to solve puzzles put before them. The first group was instructed to repeat a phrase, such as, "I will solve the puzzle." This group was testing the idea that self-affirmations increase optimism and motivation. The second group was instructed to ask themselves, "Will I solve the puzzle?" The second group solved 50 percent more puzzles than the first. It seems that asking the question activates the growth mindset that leads to problem-solving. It creates a thinking pattern that is searching for answers, patterns, and other related thoughts that help create our own motivation.

Strengths and Optimism

One of the most effective ways to build self-efficacy and optimism is to work and live in your strengths. Psychological strengths can be seen as built-in capacities for thoughts, feelings, and behaviors. When you engage one of your core strengths, you feel a sense of authenticity. It's your true self. You may even experience a higher level of energy. Using your strengths is the opposite of tiring; it's engaging.

The research is rich with studies that show how using your strengths in new ways leads to higher levels of happiness and satisfaction with life. In one study of more than 12,000 participants led by the late Chris Peterson, PhD, it was discovered that certain strengths were highly correlated with life satisfaction: love, hope, curiosity, and zest.[10] This is interesting but can leave people who do not have any of these in their top strengths feeling confused and left out.

The other approach that has been recommended as the result of several studies is that simply identifying your top strengths and using them in new ways leads to higher levels of happiness and engagement with lower levels of depressive symptoms. Although this approach has merit, it is incredibly simplistic and does not take context into account. In one review of the literature, a team of psychologists (Robert Biswas-Diener, Todd Kashdan, and Gurpal Minhas) proposes a slightly more sophisticated approach to using your strengths that can attract greater benefits to the individual.[11]

The approach has three major points. First, consider the idea that your strengths are not fixed or hard-wired since birth. Some of the earlier literature on strengths may not have gone so far as to explicitly say that strengths were a fixed part of your personality, but they certainly did lean in that direction. For instance, one set of authors introduces the concept of strengths by talking about how we create "super highways" in our brains in the first 10 years of our lives. They infer that these highways are the blueprints for our talents and that trying to build new ones is really a waste of effort. In fact, they urge people *not* to complete their strengths assessment more than once.[12] Another set of researchers concedes that there is a substantial "genetic composition" to our strengths development.[13] These claims are not outwardly false, but they lead us in a direction of thinking that says we are *stuck* with who we are in terms of our strengths. In the short term, it can be very pleasant and intriguing to learn what your top strengths are based on an assessment, but this can be followed by a period of stagnation. The research shows that there is a fair amount of variability in our personalities, both over time and between the situations that present themselves to us.[14] Simply thinking that our strengths are fixed may lead to thinking of ourselves as hammers and seeing all of our problems as nails. A more effective way of looking at our strengths may be to regulate their use based on the circumstances.

The second concept put forth by Biswas-Diener, Kashdan, and Minhas is that our strengths do not necessarily exist in isolation. They argue that using your strengths in combinations leads to the best results. Consider the psychological strengths of Gratitude and Love. According to the researchers at *VIAcharacter.org*, the strength of Gratitude is defined as "Being aware of and thankful for the good things that happen; taking time to express thanks." The strength of Love is defined as "Valuing close relations with others, in particular those in which sharing and caring are reciprocated; being close to people." Imagine that these strengths were identified as being two of your most valued. On their own, they can produce feelings of elation, connection (to the universe and others), and authenticity. When combined, however, they are powerful tools for effectiveness. A person wielding these strengths, for instance, can express his appreciation for a coworker's efforts with deep, heartfelt sincerity. Higher levels of trust, connection, and cooperation emerge and the organization benefits as well.

And the benefits of using your strengths do not stop there. Additional studies show that strengths used by research participants led to less stress, greater self-esteem, and higher levels of positive emotions. All of these elements allow us to manage ourselves more effectively through adversity and build the intrinsic belief that we are capable. In my years of coaching executives and working with corporate teams, however, this is where many have trouble connecting the dots. When an employee is disorganized or lacking adequate communication skills, the company can simply send him off to training to "fix" a weakness.

When it comes to strengths, we don't normally think about investing in an area that is already performing well.

Once many hear about this idea of focusing on their strengths, they immediately say, "Okay, sounds pretty good, but now what?" This is where Ryan Niemiec, PhD, the education director of the Values in Action Institute on Character comes in. Niemiec has developed a simple model for making your strengths come to life: Aware–Explore–Apply.

- **Aware.** Just about any self-improvement process starts with building some awareness. In this case, find a way to identify your strengths. Ask your friends, your family, and your coworkers to tell you what they see as your top strengths. Be sure to ask for examples. Or take the VIA Survey for free at *VIAcharacter.org*. It's 120 questions and you get your results immediately.
- **Explore.** Ponder your results. Which ones are surprises? Which of these are not a surprise? When can you remember using them? How have you used them to overcome an obstacle or adversity?
- **Apply.** Start mindfully applying your strengths to your work and personal life. Which strength(s) can help you solve a problem you are facing right now? Which strength(s) do you typically go to when you're feeling anxious, scared, or stressed? What goals are you pursuing to which you can apply your strengths?[15]

This all sounds great (and it is), but can we put too much focus on our strengths? I believe so and there are three basic things to watch for when making a shift to the strengths focus: disregarding your weaknesses, overusing your strengths, and missing your goals.

One of the main declarations of the strengths movement is to get the focus on strengths and off of our weaknesses. One way to define a weakness is an area in which performance is low and it drains our energy. The key in deciding if the weakness needs attention is around impact. That is, if the impact of the weakness is low or non-existent, it probably does not require a fair amount of attention. For instance, if you were hired as a software engineer to write code and do this mostly on your own, a fear of public speaking probably has no impact on your current role. So, spending time working on this may not be the best use of your limited time.

The other potential issue with strengths is that sometimes we create blind spots for ourselves. Working and living in your strengths feels good. Your energy level goes up and you get more done. The belief in your abilities soars and your levels of optimism follow. And this is where the problem lies. Since it feels so good, we focus only on those traits.

One of my top strengths according to the VIA Survey is "judgment," which the assessment defines as, "Thinking things through and examining them from all sides are important aspects of who you are. You do not jump to conclusions, and you rely only on solid evidence to make your decisions. You are able to change your mind." Years ago while running a small startup company I faced a very difficult decision almost the minute that I joined the organization. A key individual on our team shared information about salaries with the rest of the group. She was unhappy with how much she was making and this was her way of turning employees against the incoming leadership group. In addition, from everything that I could gather, she was the key person on our most important project with our most important client. The client was threatening to back out and that would have spelled doom for our tiny company.

In retrospect, I believe the company would have benefitted from her being fired almost immediately and we could have completed the project with some very long nights. But I kept looking at the situation from all sides. On one hand, she held the keys to this project and was leading several others. I was also unsure how the rest of the staff viewed her contributions. She had intimate knowledge about our technology, content, and clients. On the other hand, this was a serious breach of trust in the corporate world and she was incredibly difficult to work with when it came to trying new ideas and receiving feedback. I waffled back and forth between these points of view, thinking that keeping an open mind was the best thing to do because it felt right. Again, I was a hammer (my strength of judgment) and I thought the situation (fire the employee or keep her) looked like a nail. In reality, the organization was craving decisiveness but I was blinded by one of my top strengths.

Finally, strengths can pose a challenge when we're actually not up to it. Remember that I am not advocating an unreal optimism that makes you blind to threats and obstacles. There are times, however, when the goal is just out of reach, the hurdles are too high, and the issues are too many to handle. In fact, there is some anecdotal evidence that when highly invested in the "strengths use" approach, not attaining goals can be more disappointing. That is, we do experience more initial optimism when engaging our strengths. We feel more self-confidence as a result and our expectations of achieving the goal make us feel that it will be easier. The disappointment may be a blow to our level of optimism in the end, and something to be aware of when looking at using your strengths.

Using Goals to Build Optimism

Another way to build self-efficacy and create more optimistic thinking is through the use of goals. Some of the best research on goals comes from Edwin Locke and Gary Latham, coauthors of *A Theory of Goal Setting and Task Performance.* The authors contend that years of research in corporate settings show that setting goals and (of course) hard work are likely to improve performance. As mentioned previously, we are tying optimism to the concept of self-efficacy. As we make progress toward our goals, we increase our self-efficacy and motivation, which can create an upward spiral.

In fact, progress isn't just good for optimism at the individual level, it's good for business. In *The Progress Principle*, Teresa Amabile and Steven Kramer argue that their data shows that even small progress in meaningful work is the most powerful motivational stimulant. When I'm coaching executives, I emphasize this fact by asking them how they can help their teams make progress, every day. Amabile and Kramer put forth that employees who move their tasks forward each day are more collegial, more motivated, and more resilient. In the end, if employees feel that the work they are doing is contributing to something larger than themselves *and* they are making progress, they experience a sense of pride while being able to meet their expectations or goals. When people feel capable, they see "difficult problems as positive challenges and opportunities to succeed."[16]

In short, goals can be good for us, assuming we put in some effort. Here are some other findings from the research on goals. Incorporate them into your life to help build your optimism muscle.

- According to the "Zeigarnik Effect," you are much more likely to recall uncompleted tasks rather than one you completed. So just get started…on something.
- When visualizing or fantasizing about your goals, focus on the process versus the outcome. It helps you apply your energy to the actual steps needed to reach the goal.
- Align your goals with what's important to you. Make sure that your goals are not being imposed on you and that they are your choice.
- Simply having goals helps us organize our time, make values-based decisions, prioritize our lives, and track our progress.
- Be cautious of implementing stretch goals. The research on their effectiveness is mixed. Instead, consider goals that are attainable. (However, we also know that the higher the goal, the more likely the person is to exhibit higher performance. So use your judgment.)
- Avoid being overwhelmed by bigger, complex goals by reorganizing them into smaller challenges (sometimes referred to as sub-goals). "Small wins" build confidence and lead to higher motivation and more action.
- Find ways to measure your progress. Constant feedback is essential to success. (Sub-goals can really help with this, too.)
- Introduce some negative thinking into your goal planning. Simply asking, "What could go wrong?" prepares you for

the effort and problem-solving required for just about any issues that may arise.

- Be careful about being too specific with your goals; they may blind you to other opportunities. We often think that the obstacles we face come at us in an unpredictable way. So do opportunities; if you are too focused on your super specific goal, you may not see the opening for a different type of achievement right in front of you.

Whenever I think about how to develop someone's optimism, I think about how this is related to self-efficacy. And when I think about self-efficacy, it brings me to greatness. I am fascinated by how a select few on this planet can be so much better than the rest of us at math, football, guitar, or jiu-jitsu. What is it that makes some great while others are left in their dust?

Daniel Coyle may have isolated a number of key findings that distinguish greatness from the ordinary in his excellent book *The Talent Code*. Coyle writes that the recipe for success in just about any domain lies in three simple elements. His research first points to deep practice. If you want to get better at something, break it into smaller pieces and immerse yourself in repeating these steps. Anybody can buy a guitar, but the best stay motivated to continue their deep practice, which happens to be the second element in Coyle's model. Many of the best start with a hero that they greatly admire. This external motivation quickly turns inward when they start saying, "I *am* a musician…artist…athlete." It turns into a future vision of themselves in which superior performance is achieved. Finally, the third element involves someone else: a master coach. The master coach focuses on the deep practice as well as the motivation. They see each of their "students" as individuals and treat them as such. They give their all in the pursuit of excellence. [17]

Achieving greatness is not necessarily a guarantee of having a high level of realistic optimism (or vice-versa), but there are some other things to consider from this research that can help build hope and optimism for even the most pessimistic people. The great ones actually look for slopes in their areas of expertise. That is, they push themselves into new areas where they are less comfortable and know they are going to make mistakes. It turns out that making mistakes may just be the single best way to learn and grow. The neural networks that we have built while developing a skill begin to fire over and over again when we make mistakes. This makes the networks stronger. "Struggle is not an option," writes Coyle, "it is a biological requirement."[18] In one study, kids who took practice tests and studied less did better than the kids who studied more (in fact, four times more!) but did not take the practice tests.

How Learning Contributes to Optimism

A couple of months after finishing *The Talent Code*, I signed up to learn some self-defense skills at a local Gracie jiu-jitsu school run by Marco Moreno. When I showed up for the first lesson, I did not even have a gi (pronounced "gee," it is the white outfit that you are probably used to seeing used in most martial arts) and I have to admit that my number-one goal was to avoid injury. Marco took me aside and told me to lie on my back. He climbed into the mount position on top of me and asked me to try and get him off. I probably outweigh Marco by 20 pounds but I couldn't get this guy off. It produced a feeling in me that was a cross between being claustrophobic and just plain hopeless. Marco eventually let me up while I struggled for air. Then we switched positions. The results were pretty much the same except instead of feeling claustrophobic and hopeless, I felt incompetent. Marco tossed me like a rag doll. We sat and talked for a short while as he explained how the Gracie Combatives program worked and how once I mastered these techniques (something like 36 different moves, each with several variations) I would be allowed to test for my blue belt. My confidence was not very high at this point but Marco assured me if I just showed up and gave it my best effort, I would see results pretty quickly.

After our initial work together, Marco kicked off the class (there were about eight of us that night) and he told everyone we would be working on the Americana Armlock, a nasty move that can really hurt the other person's shoulder if done correctly. Marco then demonstrated the move with his partner (the fake bad guy) step by step. The attention to detail was amazing. He talked about how our thumbs should be positioned when we grab the "bad guy's" wrist, how our one knee needed to come out to form a base, and how the other leg made a "hook" to secure our position. Each "slice" was demonstrated several times and we probably watched the entire move five or six times before we practiced it just like we saw it. This continued all through the hour-long practice and each variation of the Americana. At the end of the class we did "reflex development" that forced us to practice the moves and their variations at a quicker pace. I must have made 50 mistakes that night but I can honestly say that I learned something and it had sunk in. After just three or four classes, I knew that if I needed to defend myself from a physical assault, I would do it very differently than what I might have done prior to this class. My belief in my abilities had increased.

Are You Lucky?

In 1971, Clint Eastwood appeared in his first *Dirty Harry* movie. He played Detective "Dirty" Harry Callahan of the San Francisco Police Department chasing a psychopathic serial killer. At one point in the movie, Callahan witnesses a bank robbery from a diner across the street. He kills two of the three robbers and wounds the third. The third ends up on the ground eyeing a loaded shotgun just a few feet away. Callahan stands over him and taunts him with: "I know what you're thinking: 'Did he fire six shots or only five?' Well, to tell you the truth, in all this excitement, I've kinda lost track myself. But being this is a .44 Magnum, the most powerful handgun in the world, and would blow your head clean off, you've got to ask yourself one question: 'Do I feel lucky?' Well, do you, punk?"

Now, think about your life for a moment. Do you feel lucky? Richard Wiseman, PhD, a psychologist at the University of Hertfordshire in the United Kingdom set up a "lucky" lab with 700 participants who had intended to buy lottery tickets. Each participant completed a questionnaire with a series of statements that measured whether the person considered themselves to be lucky or unlucky. As you could imagine, those who saw themselves as lucky were twice as confident that they would win the lottery, but there was no difference in winnings between the two groups.[19] It turns out that luck had no bearing on their ability to influence events outside of their control, so why did some feel lucky while others did not?

Wiseman discovered that the lucky ones viewed the world in a more optimistic way and then behaved in a way that was very different from the unlucky peers. Wiseman's research points to the idea that lucky people generate their own good fortune with four basic principles: "They are skilled at creating and noticing chance opportunities, make lucky decisions by listening to their intuition, create self-fulfilling prophesies via positive expectations, and adopt a resilient attitude that transforms bad luck into good."[20]

One experiment run by Wiseman demonstrates this masterfully. Much like the study with lottery tickets, he had a lucky group and an unlucky group. Both were given the same task. They were handed a newspaper and asked to count the number of photographs in the newspaper before them. On average, the unlucky people took about two minutes to complete the task while the lucky people completed the assignment in just seconds. On the second page of the newspaper (in big, bold print) was a message that read: "Stop counting; there are 43 photographs in this newspaper." It was basically staring everyone in the face. Those who considered themselves to be lucky were much more likely to see the unexpected notice about the number of photos.[21] People who consider themselves to be unlucky are generally going to be more tense and anxious and research has shown that anxiety can disrupt a person's ability to notice the unexpected.

These people don't turn their lives around by flicking a switch to be more optimistic or positive in their thinking. Besides being able to see more information, lucky people *behave* differently as well. To open themselves up to new opportunities they vary their routes to work. They engage in conversations with strangers at Starbucks and they read articles about topics they know nothing about. Lucky people know that they increase their chances of seeing the world differently (taking a different route to work) and making new friends (talking to strangers) by creating chance opportunities.

Another area in which lucky people outperform unlucky people is when they experience bad luck. When something unfortunate happens to a lucky person, they are inclined to reframe the event to see it in a more positive light. In another Wiseman study, participants are asked to imagine they are standing in a bank and suddenly an armed robber walks in and shoots them in the arm. The unlucky people might say, "Yes, that's just my luck! I'm a magnet for bad things happening." The lucky people, on the other hand, might say, "I'm feeling lucky that I was only shot in the arm. Maybe I could sell my story!" Feeling lucky allows you to see adversity in a way that also allows you to have a bright outlook for the future. The upward spiral continues.

Failure Leads to Success

Another unconventional way to build your optimism is to embrace failure. On the face of it, this seems like the opposite of the optimistic thinking we're used to when we expect things to work out. Failure and adversity are inevitable in life. Thinking you are going to get the promotion you've been seeking for the past year probably makes you more likely to get it. Recognizing that it might not happen and being willing to learn from it if it does not happen is a critical skill. Optimistic thinking is probably the most powerful after an adversity.

This sounds easier than it really is. And let's not forget that "context matters" with failure as well. If you're a cardiologist in a life-or-death surgery, I would not ask you to *embrace* failure. Unfortunately, highly trained people (like cardiologists) make mistakes and the ones that are not devastated from failure find ways to learn and become better at their craft. In other situations we encounter every day, such as cooking dinner, interviewing job candidates, running meetings, and coaching little league teams, the stakes are not necessarily life-or-death. In these situations, we may actually benefit more in the long run from failure. In fact, many of the entrepreneurs in Silicon Valley that brought us Facebook, Google, Uber, and other incredible technologies actually look for ways to fail *quickly*. By trying something that is low-cost and fails quickly, a business can remove that option from its product development list. Knowing that failure is just around the corner opens you up to less disappointment and more of a curious mindset to learn from your mistakes. Dweck's research at Stanford regarding mindsets went a step further with kids in the classroom. She found that kids who had learning goals actually outperformed kids who were striving for As or Bs. It turns out that seeking an A, for instance, may make one avoid taking on more difficult material. When the focus is on learning, failure and mistakes are an afterthought.

Here are some other interesting ideas with regard to failure and its impact on our optimism and self-efficacy.

- Mistakes force us to slow down and contemplate our goals, our processes, and our performance. Success makes us go faster.
- Most people don't read the instructions on a new product. They prefer to act and reflect on their progress.
- Hope can actually impede adaptation. If you are truly stuck with a permanent situation that does not meet your expectations, find a way to live with it.
- People who are willing to fail are more likely to take calculated risks and, therefore, achieve more.

Hopefully, some of this can help you think differently about failure and how it is a natural part of life and the progress toward an important goal. Robert Biswas-Diener, author of *The Courage Quotient,* helps us understand the most important element of coping with risk and failure: courage. Biswas-Diener offers a simple yet intelligent way of thinking of courage by imagining it as a math equation:

COURAGE QUOTIENT = (WILLINGNESS TO ACT / FEAR)

The book contains numerous strategies to increase courage, and one of the main points is that this is a skill to be acquired. Looking at it as an equation helps make it "solveable" and it gives us a target. We can focus on our willingness to act or reducing fear.[22]

Jennifer, the mother of two children with severe handicaps lives this principle out. She conjured up the courage to leave her first husband and raise the kids on her own. Jennifer barely knew how to use a screw driver. Once she was on her own, she saw home improvement projects as a way to develop herself. She overcame her fear and learned she was ready to handle any adversity.

Avoiding Extremes

Optimism is one of the trickiest topics in all of psychology. Not enough of it leads to one feeling helpless and overwhelmed. When this happens, effort pretty much disappears. Too much of it and overconfidence sets in. This leads to poor planning and missed expectations that can be equally defeating. And setting this up as a battle between two extremes is not healthy either. It is a false argument similar to the "either/or" dichotomy proposed in the previous chapter. What seems to work is the right amount of optimistic or pessimistic thinking at the right time. Overall, we do benefit with a slightly optimistic view of our lives and a true belief in our abilities to master the environment. Although we may have a tendency as a species to be overly optimistic, it does serve us well.

Paradoxes can be confusing but they can also help us see the nuance that is necessary to navigate a world that seems to throw curveballs at us from time to time. Dan Porter reminded me of the Stockdale Paradox. Dan recently wrote to me: "The longest held high-ranking POW in American history, Admiral Stockdale, was once asked who struggled the most in the POW Camps. His answer was...the Optimists. The ones who said, 'We'll be out by summer,' 'We'll be home for Thanksgiving,' and 'We'll be released for Christmas.' As those moments came and went, the optimist suffered. The Stockdale Paradox states the importance of believing we shall prevail in the end, whenever that end comes. My optimism is that life has purpose and meaning; although shrouded from us at times, it is there. Knowing that increases my patience for the temporal aspects of struggle."

Take It or Leave It

- Journal about your day with an eye on your level of optimism. How did your level of optimistic or pessimistic thinking serve your goals? What would you do differently if given the chance to relive the day?
- When intense negative thinking enters your mind, consider picturing a big stop sign. Then, distract yourself with something healthy like a conversation with a trusted friend, exercising, or reading something interesting.
- Think about the different areas of your life: work, romantic relationships, friendships, family, hobbies, and physical health. Write about your level of optimism in each of these domains and look for patterns. Where would being more optimistic or pessimistic help you?
- Ask friends, family, and colleagues to give you feedback on your personal brand as it relates to optimism. Do they think you blame yourself too often (personalization)? Do they believe that you make issues permanent versus temporary? Does an adversity in one area of your life seem to affect other areas (pervasiveness)?
- Go to *www.MindsetOnline.com* and take Carol Dweck's free mindset assessment. Consider the research that points to the advantages of a growth mindset.
- Create a goal. Make sure it is aligned with your most important values. Make the goal realistic and then make it a little harder. Break it down into smaller goals and find a way to measure progress every day, if possible.
- Create a "hero" notebook. Identify people who you admire and write about the attributes they possess that you would like to develop.
- When faced with an adversity, avoid talking to yourself with positive affirmations. Instead, ask yourself, "Can I do it? How can I do it?"

- Go to *www.VIAcharacter.org* and take the 20-minute strengths assessment. Find ways to work your top strengths into your life in new behaviors and thought patterns.
- Before you go to sleep, think about (better yet, write about) your small wins. Were you able to juggle a demanding job with planning and making dinner for your family? Did you complete a presentation for your manager? Get creative.
- Upon waking up in the morning, think about your day and all the things you need to do. Then, identify the one thing that you can complete that will add the most value to your life. Write this down and make sure to cross it off at night.
- Take up a hobby. Find something enjoyable and meaningful to you. Put time on your calendar to engage this hobby.
- Think about how lucky you really are. Find ways to act on this luck by taking a new route to work, changing who you talk to at parties, or find new people with whom you can network that you wouldn't normally approach.
- Take small bets and get ready to fail. Focus on learning as much as possible from the experience versus being successful in conventional measures. Take action.

5

Mindfulness and Curiosity Make a Comeback

There is nothing either good or bad but thinking makes it so.

—William Shakespeare

A number of years ago, I was talking to a friend of mine about a relationship that was creating a great deal of stress for me. Emails from this person sent my heart rate through the roof and conversations with this person were worse. I could feel a lump in my throat and my palms would get sweaty. My sympathetic nervous system would kick in automatically when we would engage in a conversation via email, text, phone, or in person. I was in fight or flight mode immediately.

My goal in the conversation with my friend was to get some advice on how to respond to several emails from "adversary." I read through each email aloud, waiting for my friend to respond. I noticed my heart rate climbing and my anger mounting just from reading these notes. After reading the emails out loud to my friend, I anticipated some very witty responses that would help me "win" these battles. He completely surprised me by saying, "Why don't you just try being curious for the next week?"

"Wait a minute. So, you don't think I should respond?" I quickly said.

"No, he replied. "Just practice being curious. Explore what this really means. Think about how this is affecting you emotionally and physically. Yes, just be curious."

A week passed before my friend and I spoke of these emails again. I spent the week being curious and not reacting. My anger cooled off. The situation really didn't need any more antagonistic communication. My life was better as a result. And so began my journey into the world of curiosity and mindfulness.

The Benefits of Curiosity

It turns out that curiosity may have killed the cat, but it has immense benefits to humans. Merriam-Webster defines curiosity as "The desire to learn or know more about something or someone." This seems accurate from an academic standpoint, but there is more to the experience of feeling curious. When we are immersed in curiosity, something happens to us. We become totally focused on that which we show interest. Our motivation increases and our brains crave more information. In his book on the same subject (*Curious?*), Todd Kashdan offers a more robust, intriguing definition. He talks about how when we recognize novelty and seize the pleasure it offers us, we also draw meaning from it.

Curiosity is also more complex than just demonstrating interest in a subject or person. It can be viewed as a tool or a resource to help us live meaningful, resilient lives. We can have moments of intense interest and curiosity. Something can pique our interest and move us to learn more. Some people are curious all the time (little kids) and some are fixed on their view of the world and show little interest beyond the world that they inhabit. In some cases, our curiosity can be so durable that it lasts a lifetime. We can turn our curiosity into a meaningful career (the author of this book). And, other times our initial high interest flames out and wanes over time.

Some of these elements can be seen in the choices we make around hobbies, careers, and even romantic partners. In my early 20s, I pursued a career in sports management. After conducting an endless number of informational interviews, sending out resumes, and applying for jobs, I landed a sales position with Reebok in the Midwest. My initial interest in the industry was quickly overcome by the fact that I spent several hours a day in my car talking to owners of small sporting goods shops about products like leotards and eccentric running gear, none of which really interested me. I had a manager who only cared about my sales. The training to do my job was non-existent and my family and friends were half a continent away. In short, it was a disaster. All of the energy that I plowed into getting the job seemed wasted. That initial high interest clouded my judgment and kept me from asking the difficult questions: What exactly would I be selling? With whom would I be working? What is the worst part of the job? Instead, I left after a few months. In the end, it helped create a better definition of the career I wanted but it was a painful journey.

Curiosity also plays a role in our relationships. When we first meet someone, we want to know everything about this person. We want to spend heaps of time with them and learn everything we can about them. Over time, we begin to predict their behaviors and reactions and the flame burns a little less bright. This is why a good friend of mine and his wife make it a habit of inviting several diverse couples over for dinner when they entertain. It makes for awkward conversations with differing views. Nothing is off-limits: politics, religion, parenting, and so on. Sometimes, he will stir the pot a little to get the debates started. When his lovely wife enters the conversation, he exercises his curiosity about how she will respond and what makes her take a particular stance. He gets to see his wife in a new light and learn something about her. It keeps the relationship fresh. Instead of assuming he knows everything about her, he knows that there is a lifetime of learning.

And, curiosity provides us with benefits, according to Kashdan. There is some initial research (please proceed with caution!) that shows that preventing or delaying Alzheimer's Disease may be impacted by exercising your curiosity.[1] In fact, the Alzheimer's Association recommends staying "curious and involved–commit to lifelong learning." (The association admits that this is not clear cut and offers that more research needs to be done in the areas of diet, sleep, stress management, and mental stimulation.)[2] The National Institutes of Health (NIH) also recommends "intellectual stimulation" such as reading books and magazines in addition to attending lectures on topics that may be of interest to you.[3] Again, the research is in its early days but it is promising.

It also turns out that curiosity may increase our ability to be attentive. When we learn something new, we automatically drop it into a category. Categories make it easier for us to recall information when we need it most. For instance, when we learn what a phone is, we scan our communication category and realize we have several options when we need to reach out to someone. So, the more we learn about the features of something new (for example, a smartphone, a math equation, and cars), we are able to focus our attention in the moment to bring up relevant information. As we learn more, we may also put things in multiple categories and see associations that can boost our creativity. At some point, someone realized that a phone could be mobile and that it could be so powerful that we would refer to it as "smart."

Speaking of being smart, many people think of the intelligence quotient (IQ) as something fixed or immutable. As mentioned earlier, Carol Dweck's research shows that people who think they can get "smarter" tend to do so with the growth mindset. She recommends that we fight this "brutal pessimism" by focusing more on the connection between effort and results.[4] People with a growth mindset are more likely to create learning goals along with trying to achieve high grades and performance. That is, they put their energy into mastering a subject instead of simply doing well on a test. And curiosity is one way to learn more. Alfred Binet, commonly known as the person who developed the first practical IQ test, didn't create it to identify those who were brilliant. He did it to identify the kids who were struggling in school and would benefit from some extra attention from their teachers.[5]

Curiosity can also help us generate meaning and purpose in our lives. For instance, simply learning more about the health effects of refined sugar adds meaning to my life. I take that knowledge and change the way I live. I share this knowledge with my kids and other adults to help them make more informed decisions about their diets. Others may find meaning paying attention to politics, climate change, or martial arts. "As long as something is novel," Kashdan says, "we are still in the process of finding and creating meaning."[6]

Finally, curiosity is highly correlated with happiness, according to several studies. In one study, participants who took the VIA Strengths Survey and found curiosity to be in their top five strengths reported higher levels of life satisfaction. In a later study, participants were given new tasks and asked to deeply explore these new activities and describe their absorption in a written report. Levels of satisfaction with life rose in these participants as well. In fact, it seemed that those who reported low levels of curiosity in their lives were most likely to benefit from this intervention.

Dealing With Anxiety

Imagine that you're really worried about something very important to you. Your best friend sees the anxiety on your face and asks what's wrong. You tell him what you're worried about and he responds with one of the following statements:

- "It'll be okay."
- "Everything always works out."
- "You'll be fine."
- "Don't worry."

It's as if your friend thinks there is a knob you can simply turn to reduce your anxiety. But what really happens when we turn this knob? Many times our anxiety goes up. It turns out that nature has played a little bit of a trick on us. We can't directly reduce our worry. That knob is not connected to anything. Right next to it, however, is a knob that controls our attention. We can direct our attention and curiosity to anything that we choose. And, by the way, when we decide to be nonjudgmentally aware and curious about something, our worry can naturally come down. When we become interested in something, our focus is not on how painful the emotions feel but how we crave more information. Our emotions become secondary to learning and acquiring knowledge.

This isn't to say that seeking the support of friends and family when we're anxious is a bad thing. It's just that the previous responses can minimize how we feel. Of course, it's much easier for someone else to say these things because they are not fully experiencing our context. They care for you but they are not you. The worry that you are experiencing is based on your perception of something important to you being at risk. Curiosity actually makes us open to experiencing any emotions as they arise. Trying to fix or suppress your anxiety is setting up a battle between something you perceive to be good and bad. As we'll discuss in the next chapter, all emotions are simply markers that help us navigate the environment.

How Rookies Leverage Curiosity

In the mid-1970s, George Lucas shopped his original version of *Star Wars* to major movie studios and producers. Once he received the initial commitment for financial backing and support, he had to put a plan in place and hire a team to create what he was referring to as a "space opera." Movie and television shows about space had been around for a number of years but Lucas wanted to take it to another level with his visual effects. When he described how he wanted to show multiple spaceships in dog fights while the camera was panning from side to side, veterans of the special effects industry told him that he could not do it. He brought his ideas to several special effects firms and got the same answer each time: It can't be done.

Lucas, not wanting to give up and knowing that there had to be a way to do this, decided to flip his assumptions about expertise. He hired a bunch of recent college graduates and threw the problems at them. In the end, it was their curiosity, passion, and interest that led to special effects the public had never seen before. They worked tireless hours. They stressed about deadlines but they never lost their curiosity for finding new ways to do things. So much of their work was novel and interesting to them that it drove their motivation to learn more each day. So it wasn't necessarily the elimination of worry that propelled them to great heights because they were under a tremendous amount of pressure; It was their intense interest and belief in themselves that enabled them to solve problems as they arose. (As I'm writing this, the *Star Wars* movies have grossed almost $6.5 billion.)

Liz Wiseman, in her book *Rookie Smarts*, argues that the new essential tools in the business world are not experience but the willingness and ability to learn.[7] A rookie is defined as someone new to a given role, so it is not necessarily a recent college graduate or an intern. It could be a senior vice president, who has spent her entire career in sales, who is asked to "clean up" customer service. This "rookie" is more likely to succeed, according to Wiseman, if she embraces her curiosity by experimenting with new ideas rather than falling back on years of knowledge and "best practices." Rookies are great at learning from their mistakes; it's expected. Veterans, on the other hand, try to hide their mistakes. Rookies are also very willing to seek counsel from others. They crave new knowledge. Veterans spend their time and energy proving they have all the knowledge. They are confident and humble at the same time.

Mindfulness and Curiosity

A close cousin of curiosity is mindfulness. And mindfulness is all the rage. Hardly a day goes by without someone forwarding me an article about how mindfulness is good for leaders, kids, parents, and everyone in between. Dozens (if not hundreds) of studies have looked at mindful practices such as meditation to see how they affect our well-being and resilience. In many cases, the results are very positive. One meta-analysis of the literature suggests that mindfulness meditation can increase positive affect, improve coping, and reduce stress. It seems there is not much that mindfulness can't help with in our desire to be happier, more effective, and more resilient.

Even though mindfulness is getting a lot of press, it is still misunderstood and, by my account, it is not being practiced by most people. Let's first define this concept before discussing the benefits and how to incorporate it in our lives. Jon Kabat-Zinn, an expert in meditation at the University of Massachusetts, defines mindfulness as "paying attention, on purpose, in the moment, nonjudgmentally." Some experts place most of their focus simply on attention. Others believe that being nonjudgmental is the key.

There are two difficulties with mindfulness: practicing it and explaining it. It's hard to convince clients to give it a try if you can't articulate exactly what it is in meaningful, practical ways. In my opinion, Eline Snel, therapist and author of *Sitting Still Like a Frog* has done exactly this. Snel wrote her book with the idea of helping parents teach mindfulness techniques to their children. Because this can be a difficult concept to fully comprehend, I see Snel's approach as being equally effective for adults as well. Even her definition of mindfulness ("deliberate, friendly attention") is simple and her recommendations are practical and easy to try.

For instance, Snel writes that wishing and desires take us away from the present moment and that we are better off when we don't believe all of our thoughts.[8] Many of our thoughts, as discussed earlier, are a mix of facts and stories. When we believe these thoughts to be absolute facts, we can create a downward spiral of emotion. Snel offers three incredibly simple, powerful thoughts for parents who observe a child not behaving as we expect.

1. **Presence.** Be completely in the present moment; recognize that focusing your attention on your laptop, tablet, or phone is not the same as being in the moment with your child (or anyone else for that matter!).
2. **Understanding.** Be curious about your child; ask why he might be acting like this. What is going on within him that could cause this behavior?
3. **Acceptance.** Witnessing the child's actions without wanting to change it may be the most difficult of the three, as most of us have very strong thoughts about how our children should act, how they need to act, and how they have to act.[9]

Once we start to become aware of our own thinking in an objective way, we realize that our minds are actually getting in the way much of the time. Just like a petulant child, the mind needs to rest. The constant judging of the world around us as good or bad is tiring. Endless worry about the future also makes us tired. And rumination about what has already taken place and cannot be changed drains us of precious energy. Mindfulness, on the other hand, can have the restorative power of a good night's sleep. After meditating, for instance, you can return to your job or to parenting with renewed vigor and even a different perspective.

We talked about the role of technology and how it gets in the way of being present. When we have our phone on the table, our thoughts drift to email, Facebook, and unread text messages. We miss out on the nuance of our partner's unexpected frown or hesitation when sharing an important story about his day. Being fully present is a gift to yourself and the person with whom you are sharing the moment.

One of the greatest attributes of the human brain is that it can be used as a powerful time machine. We can instantly zip back 30 years to our high school days and think about the state championship we (almost) won. Or, we can look at someone on a first date and imagine what life would be like if we decided to get married and have kids. From what we know about the animal kingdom, this is a uniquely human capability. We can fly backward or forward and immediately drop into an experience of joy, sorrow, hope, and awe. This human time machine can also be used to our detriment.

According to the research of Matt Killingsworth and Daniel Gilbert of Harvard University, our minds wander almost 50 percent of the time (46.9 percent to be exact).[10] And when they wander, they usually produce less happiness than when they are present. They argue that wandering may be the default state and that contemplating the past and considering the future are just what we do. (Having sex was the one activity that produced the least meandering.) They also posit that a very small percentage of our happiness can be gained from the specific activity we're engaged in (4.6 percent) while our mind wandering status is responsible for about 10.8 percent of our mood.[11] Living in the moment, it turns out, is a good strategy for our well-being.

Looking at it from another point of view, the current moment is all that really matters. The past does not really exist, nor does the future. The only thing that we can verify is the present moment, yet we focus entirely too much energy fixated on what happened yesterday and what might happen tomorrow. This is not to say that we should not plan for retirement and college. And we can certainly learn from the past.

According to the research of Phil Zimbardo, retired professor at Stanford University, there are several ways to treat time.[12] We can be focused on the past, the present, or the future. Each of these time perspectives can be either positive or negative. For instance, I look at my childhood as an incredibly positive experience. My parents provided me and my sisters with shelter, healthy food, and their full attention, and I think I speak for my sisters when I say that I never questioned my parents' love and devotion to our well-being. Others, unfortunately, may focus their memories on parents who were inattentive, riddled with debt, and emotionally distant. I am also fortunate enough to think about my future in a very positive way. I plan to stay connected to my sons, write more books, engage with loved ones, take on new hobbies, and grow my business. Others may take a more negative approach to the future by thinking that terrorism will get worse, economic ruin is inevitable, and climate change will wipe us out. Finally, we can enjoy the present, something Zimbardo refers to as being hedonistic. For me, I might indulge in an episode of *Seinfeld*, go for a run, or eat a doughnut. The optimal time perspective is a mix of all three. Being positively oriented toward the past, having a moderate hedonistic bent, and a moderate future-positive orientation seems to be best. So it's not that we abandon the past or future, but not accounting for the present can rob us of so many wonderful moments. Too much orientation on the past or future and we miss the beautiful sunset, our child snuggling up next to us on the couch, and even the complement from the vice-president for our outstanding effort on a recent project.

Another nice trick that our minds play on us is "judging." We typically assess things as good or bad as they are presented to us. It's an almost automatic reaction. We are taught that somewhere in the first 30 seconds of meeting someone that both parties are forming long-lasting opinions of others (for example, you never get a second chance to make a first impression). We are judging machines. We label things as good and bad just as we fill in the missing details with our stories. When we are truly mindful, we suspend our judgment. We re-perceive our context in a way that allows us to dispassionately observe both the situation and what's happening in our mind. As an executive coach, I am trained to suspend my judgment so that I can provide objectivity to my clients. I am more likely to see things as they are while my clients might be a victim of their stories and emotions. We all have the capability to be our own coaches when we suspend our judgment. Once we do this, we shift our perspective, which makes us more effective to cope with a given adversity.

In order to suspend our judgment, objectifying our thoughts is key. Consider this statement: "I am angry." One way to read this is that you *are* an angry person. Technically, it is a permanent statement about our state of mind. It is also defining you. I am Polish, German, French, and a host of other nationalities. This is who *I am*; it never changes. It's in my blood and defines me.

I offer my clients another way of talking about their emotions. They might say something like: "I am experiencing thoughts of anger right now." There are several ways that saying something like this is different and, perhaps, more mindful. First, phrasing your emotional state like this creates objectivity. You are experiencing the anger, but it is not who you are in total. The goal is to create some detachment from your emotions so that you can see them for what they are: feelings that can cloud your observations. Eckhart Tolle, author of *The Power of Now*, writes that being mindful allows us to "disidentify" with the mind.[13] Once we get comfortable with this idea, we start to view our minds as we did when we were children and we stop taking ourselves too seriously. The second element of the updated phrase is the lack of permanence. By ending the thought with "right now," it sends a signal to our conscious self that these feelings (like all that we experience) are temporary. This can be a powerful reminder when intense negativity has its grip on us.

Being Present and Objective

Shortly after the conversation with my very wise friend about the relationship that was troubling me, I started making daily efforts to be more mindful by engaging in a few minutes of meditation each morning, taking walks during which I paid attention to nature, and stopped working several times a day to focus on my heartbeat or on my breath.

Mindfulness and curiosity became habits for me. And about six months later, my adversary and I had an incredibly productive conversation. In fact, my heart rate did not rise. There was no sweating (at least on my part) and we found a solution to our disagreement that was not possible just a few months earlier. I told my friend who had offered me the advice about being curious and he said, "Yes, your brain has changed." There is a growing mountain of research pointing to the fact that practicing mindfulness is essential to our overall mental health and resilience, particularly in our over-connected, over-scheduled, change-dominated society.

I love technology. I love gadgets and apps that help me increase my productivity. I have Apple TV. I'm writing this on a MacBook Air and I don't go anywhere without my Samsung Note 3. As many of you know, today's smartphones are more powerful than the computers that guided our astronauts to land on the moon. They perform the simplest of functions, like a calculator or a watch. And they have evolved to take voice commands and turn them into movie tickets. My phone even alerts me to heavy traffic and nudges me to leave early for appointments with clients. Information has become so easy to retrieve that we now take pride in our ability to multi-task. In fact, it has become a badge of honor where I live (northern Virginia) to be busy and juggle lots of things at once. Technology definitely makes it easier to be busy, but is it good for us? Or does it sap our resilience?

There are several issues at play when it comes to resilience, technology, and mindfulness. The first is information, the second is time, and the third is connection. Just think about how much information you are presented with on a daily basis. You receive emails, texts, and notifications from sites like Instagram, Facebook, and LinkedIn. I have no problem with any of these apps. I consider all technology to be neutral. It's how we use it that makes a difference in our lives. For instance, allowing your phone to beep and/or vibrate with every new notification is a recipe for being a slave to your phone.

Just this past weekend, I attended my younger son's travel basketball game. As a custom, one parent from each team is asked to volunteer and run the clock and keep score in the official book. I got there a little late and ended up being assigned to run the clock, which included changing the score as each team made a layup, free throw, or a jump shot. I took the job seriously and put my full attention on the game and my duties. The parent from the other team told me that she had done this many times before. Very early in the game, I noticed that she was texting someone while the game was in play. Several times, she asked me who scored or who received a foul so that she could record the information accurately. At one point in the fourth quarter, however, there was a discrepancy between the score that I had on the electronic board and what she had recorded in the book. Keep in mind that her son was playing and that she had given up several hours of her own personal time to invest in him, yet she was tethered to her phone. She couldn't keep her hands off of it.

This, of course, is not uncommon. When I facilitate a corporate workshop with multiple participants, many are not aware that I see them tapping away on iPhones underneath the table. Some tell me they are under immense pressure with a looming deadline while others don't even feel the need to acknowledge the pact we made at the beginning of the class to stay off of our phones. When this occurs, I usually pull out the following story told to me by a very good friend.

> About 20 years ago, we were hit with a brutal snowstorm. My driveway was about 50 to 60 yards in length. Luckily, I had invested in a snow blower, but it was still pretty hard work. I spent hours moving snow and had to repeat the process several times. I went to bed pretty early but woke up around 1 a.m. I thought I would see if the snow was still falling so I quietly walked over to the window, careful not to disturb my wife's sleep. When I looked out the window, my jaw must have hit the ground. I stood there transfixed looking out over my driveway to see nothing but snow. It looked as if I had not touched it. The combination of more heavy snowfall and strong winds had obliterated my progress. It was then that I realized how insignificant I really was.

This story stops people dead in their tracks. Mindfulness, in one respect, when practiced at its deepest levels, brings forth a humility that helps us shed some of the burdensome expectations we create for ourselves. When a lack of humility is present, we tend to overestimate the level of our importance. We can disregard agreed-upon group norms to check our phones because *we are really important*. This can be tiring and lead to mindless behaviors.

Rener Gracie is a fourth-degree black belt in Gracie Jiu-Jitsu and the co-creator of Gracie University. He and his brother Ryron developed a curriculum to help students master the techniques that have been a part of their family for almost 100 years. Rener believes that mindfulness plays a role in our lives as well as on the mat in what he calls "the most effective martial art in the world." On the mat, mindfulness helps you see the moment for what it is. If you are grappling with an opponent and find that you are in a difficult position, instead of punishing yourself for allowing this to happen, being nonjudgmental helps you identify a move that can put you in a better position. In life off of the mat, Rener believes that mindfulness can be an asset in our interactions with others. When someone is perceived as being disrespectful, instead of "boiling over," he pauses to reflect on the moment. "I am able to respond more effectively when I reflect on their situation," Rener says. And he adds, "Being mindful teaches you humility so that you refrain from taking the offensive with their offenses." When we think we are the center of the universe, we tend to make ourselves more vulnerable to being offended. We start to see the missteps of others as being directed toward us. We start to think that projects and teams can't survive without us. All of this adds to the weight of very busy lives.

Technology can fool us into thinking we can manage our time effectively. It provides a false sense of security in that we can put events in neat, 30-minute or one-hour increments on a calendar with invitations, notifications, and even travel time reminders. Most (if not all) of the executives that I coach and the various people who attend our workshops have very little free time during normal business hours. Many will have back-to-back meetings for the entire day. They grab lunch on the run and are notoriously late for every meeting. They catch up on emails during meetings or late at night. Some now get up extra early to "do work" before most people arrive. It does not stop there, as their families have activities, as well. Kids are carted off in different directions for basketball or soccer practice. In some cases, kids are even going to two practices in one day, as they are committed to multiple teams in one season. We learn about how to over-schedule ourselves at a very early age now.

The most successful executives are those who have learned how to say no to activities, invitations, and tasks that do not add value to their lives. One study cited by *Harvard Business Review* claims that employees who actually take all of their vacation time are *more likely* to be promoted.[14] Overall, Americans are taking less time off than at any other time in the last 40 years. Of course, not all vacations are created equally. In fact, on one vacation I recently took with some friends, it was hard not to notice how often everyone was on their phones, at their laptops, or joining a "mandatory" conference call. I know that times have changed, but I cannot imagine my dad taking a work call on vacation when we were kids. Of course, this could have changed with a smartphone, but I can also say that we had his (and my mom's) full attention.

The founders of Asana, an enterprise collaboration software company with more than $38 million in venture capital funding, feel that mindfulness is at the heart of their success.[15] (The company's name is even taken from a yoga pose!) Mindfulness, in their opinion, offers benefits to both individuals and organizations. They don't just focus on productivity. They believe that being mindful promotes seeing everyone as human beings, not robots. Productivity is still important and it requires a great deal of energy. Being mindful makes room for rest and reflection. It helps you redirect your limited energy in ways that serve your purpose and most valued goals.

Mindfulness and Multi-Tasking

Why do many people feel overwhelmed and burned out at work now more than ever? Multi-tasking is surely one of the main culprits. For some reason, we believe that we can do more than one thing at a time. Multi-tasking blurs the lines between tasks, reduces the sense of accomplishment, increases mistakes, and decreases energy. Students who send text messages during class or check Facebook get lower grades, on average. And research from Stanford University shows that we pay another price for multi-tasking. Their study offers that it lowers attention span and seems to affect short-term memory.[16] (On a humorous note, multi-taskers think they are really good at it, but it turns out that those with a preference for doing one thing at a time are actually better at multi-tasking than the multi-taskers!) Still another study shows an actual drop in IQ for those who multi-task. A 15-point drop essentially turned men in the study into 8-year-old boys.[17] Multi-tasking doesn't just harm you in the moment. It seems to have long-lasting effects. That is, multi-taskers have trouble ignoring irrelevant data even when they are not doing three things at once. They see something new and they attend to it, then they are on to the next thing. As a result, their memory may be poorer as a result.

Science seems to be telling us that trying to do more than one thing at a time is a recipe for mistakes and feeling overwhelmed. Even the term "multi-tasking" is inaccurate. What we're really doing is switching between tasks. And for anyone who has ever tried to write a paper, a blog post, or a book, you know that stopping to answer the phone, talk to a child, or look at an email has a high cost. We lose our train of thought. We go back and re-read what we just wrote and try to remember the basic point.

And this is all well and good. So we have some data that confirms our multi-tasking ways are harmful to us in the short and long terms. The bigger impact is on our relationships. If we believe we can do two things at once, it might just include checking email and talking to someone. My nephew recently told me that one of his college professors loved his Apple Watch because it allowed him to casually glance at his wrist while speaking with someone else to check his email. The professor thought this was a good thing because the other person wouldn't know he was not paying attention. Just as importantly, kudos to my nephew for realizing this was a bad idea.

Besides providing us with peace and serenity, mindfulness in the right dose at the right time can make us more effective at solving problems and successfully coping with adversity. The ability to *see* the moment for what it really is requires us to be *in* the moment. Checking email, ruminating about your mistakes, and worrying about the future prevent you from taking a seat in the present to observe the current situation fully. Suspending our judgment can provide us with enormous benefits. Holding the notion that our initial stories are flawed allows us to see things more clearly. It actually opens up *more* options for us versus the typical fight or flight response.

Mindfulness has a very interesting role with our emotions as well. As mentioned earlier, curiosity is one antidote to being overly worried or anxious about the future. It puts you in a position to be open to new information. In fact, you want more of it, whereas anxiety usually shuts this process down. Being mindful takes it one step further. If we feel anxiety creeping up on us, making the decision to be in the moment and nonjudgmental allows us to *accept* our reality. An old colleague of mine used to respond to my complaining at work with, "It is what it is." Years ago, it used to make me angry. It almost felt good to complain. But what I realized (years later) was that he was asking me to recognize that there are forces outside of our control that have brought this situation to us. More importantly, I believe he was also trying to help me understand that the sooner I accepted the reality of the situation, the sooner I could select the best course of action.

So many self-help gurus and books are teaching us to rid ourselves of stress, anxiety, and anger. (Even the title of this book might influence you to think those things are bad!) Mindfulness teaches us to stop making this a battle. Simply accepting you are angry with your colleagues and recognizing this emotion reduces its power over you. My youngest son is all about sports. As of the writing of this book, he is focused on playing basketball and flag football. There is not a day that goes by that he doesn't say, "Dad, do you want to throw the football?" Last year, our team made it to the championship game. Right after an energy-packed breakfast, he started getting ready and I noticed he was not his talkative self. He said, "Dad, I'm *really* nervous. I feel like throwing up." I paused and asked if he knew why he was nervous. He talked about making mistakes, losing the game, and possibly letting his teammates down. I didn't discount what he said and I offered another way to look at his anxiety. I told him that these feelings were simply telling him that the game was important to him. We talked about being curious about his thoughts and the feeling in his belly. Before I knew it, he was back and ready to play. (We won the championship in a nail-biter, in case you're curious!)

Meaning and Purpose

Since the beginning of time, people have been asking, "What is the meaning of life?" I am not going to attempt an answer because I believe it is different for each person. And according to the research, when we're mindful, we experience more moments of meaning and are more likely to recognize our own, individual purpose in life. Recognizing our purpose allows us to invest in something larger than ourselves. Purpose helps us set big goals that energize and challenge us. We see the connection between hard work and success. The paradox, of course, is that if we get too focused on goals, we don't live in the present moment any longer. Being mindful, from time to time, helps you come back to reality. In a peaceful, thoughtful way, you can objectively see if your current goals and progress are still aligned with who you are and who you want to be. And keep in mind your purpose can change.

When Marilyn Frazier was in her 20s, her sole purpose was to raise three healthy, educated children into successful adults. Now, she is focused on her work with a charity and being a grandmother. She wrote to me about mindfulness in her own life: "When I was raising my children, I was too worried about the present and the future to fully enjoy the moment. Now I tell parents to enjoy this time by being fully engaged with their children because time goes very quickly and they grow up fast." Marilyn may have been stressed about her kids' safety, driving them to different ball fields, and making sure they earned good grades, but she was never overwhelmed. Her sense of purpose gave her confidence that she could make it work.

Daniel Porter feels strongly about mindfulness and how it is connected to his resilience. He says:

> Mindfulness is the key that unlocks meaning. I am not as mindful as I'd like to be, but when I am, it is the golden thread binding all meaning. As a writer, mindfulness feeds my creativity. It's the recognition of the movement of life energy, allowing that movement to inspire curiosity, wonder, relevance, and

> insight, which I seek to share back through my writing. One of the favorite passages I ever penned came in my early twenties. I remember exactly where I sat, exactly the scene in nature I was watching, I remember exactly how my body felt and the energy coursing through me. That's mindfulness to me.[18]

And, of course, there is a study that finds people who experience more meaning and purpose might even...wait for it...live longer.[19]

Meaning and purpose help us bounce back from adversity by getting us to focus on what is really important. A colleague of mine just ended a nasty divorce that left her in debt, facing a lawsuit, and worrying about how to raise two beautiful children on her own. Now, when a client cancels their work and one of her employees misses a deadline, it looks insignificant to her. Her purpose is to provide for her kids. She still has her moments and she still excels at work, but there is an overall sense of peace with her that I have not seen in some time. She claims it is her purpose. I must agree.

As we discussed in the earlier chapters, you can have too much of a good thing. And so it is with mindfulness. One study at Georgetown University found that those with higher levels of mindfulness experienced lower levels of implicit learning on some tasks.[19] Being two open and aware to stimuli may make it harder to form habits (both good and bad). Mindfulness is about bringing the present moment up from our subconscious to our conscious mind. These moments of full lucidity can be inefficient. Think of a major league baseball player being fully conscious as a 95-mile-per-hour fastball comes toward home plate. Or think of a well-seasoned sales executive giving an important, passionate plea to a potential client. Both probably benefit more from some level of habitual automaticity.

As Kashdan and Biswas-Diener ask in *The Upside of Your Dark Side*, what would life be like if you didn't spend time reminiscing about the past?[20] Imagine not experiencing any regret or hope. We would learn less, make more tragic mistakes, and be less likely to even set meaningful goals. Shutting off with a little mindlessness each day can be very restful. A good *Seinfeld* or *Modern Family* with my kids can be all I need after a long day. Mindfulness, like the other skills, is most useful to you when you wield it with the precision of a laser versus the indiscriminate sledgehammer. Living a mindful life is not a bad idea, as long as you recognize that you are human and fallible. Being kind to yourself and forgiving makes mindfulness possible. Being mindless and expressing anger, jealousy, hope, awe, greed, and joy make you a more interesting person.

Take It or Leave It

- The next time you feel the urge to change something that really bothers you (your child's behavior, traffic on your way to work, or your manager's priorities), just be curious about it. What might my child be feeling right now? What caused the traffic? How did my manager come to these conclusions? Suspend your judgment of the answers you identify.
- Practice being curious about something that does not interest you. Find an angle in this subject and explore.
- Commit time each day to being curious about a subject you love. Find a new way to learn about it. If you're not the type of person who can sit down with a 200-page book, do a Google search or get a subscription to a magazine on the topic. Go to *Ted.com* and search for your topic or sign up for my newsletter at *http://bit.ly/DRHgroup* where I review a different book each month (so you don't have to read it).
- Identify your assumptions about a given issue you are facing. View your mind like a petulant child and laugh at your assumptions.
- Find a role in which you can be a "rookie." For me, it was Gracie Jiu-Jitsu. The first day on the mat I knew less than everyone in attendance. I had no choice but to be curious and accept that I would make a lot of mistakes.
- Read *The Power of Now* by Eckhart Tolle. Take notes and read it very slowly.
- Download an app to your smartphone that guides you through a meditation. There are dozens of free apps for both Apple and Android phones.
- For the first several bites of each meal, be mindful of the food as it enters your mouth. Think about how you would describe it to an alien who had never had food from our planet. Describe its texture, temperature, and taste.

- Do a body scan several times a day. Find a comfortable place to sit. Close your eyes and pay attention to your breath while inhaling and exhaling at least five times. Starting at your feet, pay attention to your body from your toes up to the top of your head. Go slowly and be curious. As your mind wanders, gently bring it back to the task at hand. Be curious and nonjudgmental.
- Observe your thoughts without judging them. When an uncomfortable thought enters your mind, resist the urge to suppress it or change the feeling. Be with it. Pay attention to the different sensations you experience in your body with each emotion.
- Pay attention to the language that you use when telling someone else about how you feel. Consider changing "I am angry" to "I am experiencing thoughts of anger." The difference is subtle and powerful at the same time. The change turns your thoughts from permanent, universal, and personal to temporary and objectified.
- Manage the notifications on your laptop, tablet, and phone. Contemplate shutting off all notifications for email, social media, and texting. These encourage interruption, multi-tasking, and mindlessness.
- When asked to do something that you normally accept, say no. Make time for rest and renewal. Create a "stop doing list" along with your "to-do list."
- Commit to doing one thing at a time. Be mindful every time you pick up your smartphone or engage in "task switching."
- Consider some of your routine tasks such as cooking dinner for your family, creating project plans for your company, and driving the kids to practice. *Make* meaning out of them. A routine dinner transforms into *providing a nutritious meal that allows your family to bond and connect.* A project plan becomes a *way for your team to add value and serve a larger purpose.* Driving the kids to practice is now

giving your precious time to the kids so they can learn about being part of a team, taking instruction from a coach, and getting exercise.

- Wear a "mindfulness bracelet." A rubber band will do. Determine which of your beliefs is getting in the way of your resilience and well-being. Each time this belief enters your mind, move the bracelet to the other hand. Avoid punishing yourself. Simply create awareness for yourself.

6

The Role of Positive and Negative Emotions

Positive emotions are the seeds of resilience.

—Barbara Fredrickson

A number of years ago, I started practicing gratitude with my sons. My younger son seemed to take to the exercise with his usual passion and eagerness to please. When I put him down to bed, I asked him to list three good things that happened to him that day. His usual response went something like this: "I played football with Gus. I had fun with my friends at school. And I got to spend time with you, Dad." The last one, no doubt, is how he simply hones his sales skills.

My older son, on the other hand, usually required a little "encouragement" to bring forth his three good things. When I entered his room, I found him with his comforter and sheets clear over his head. My standard response was to tickle him until the comforter and sheets came back down and then we would hear the good things that happened to him. On one particularly difficult day in the midst of my divorce, I walked into his room to find him under the covers. But this time, I did not have the energy to tickle him, so I kissed him on the forehead through the blankets. I turned and walked away. When I was about halfway to the bedroom door, I heard the swish of the sheets come back down and his sweet little voice: "Dad, what about three good things?"

This story demonstrates one of the basic principles of positive emotions: They feel good. As it turns out, my son didn't really need to be coerced into practicing gratitude. It felt good to him, along with the connection that it brought between us. Therein lies the rub with what Barbara Fredrickson, PhD, has proven with her research. As director of the Positive Emotions and Physiology (PEP) Lab at the University of North Carolina, Fredrickson's research is quoted far and wide by those who espouse that more positive emotions are better. To her credit, Fredrickson recognizes that there is nuance to the role of positivity in our lives. Years ago, she offered a simple ratio as a guidepost for how much positivity we should be experiencing versus the amount of negativity. A couple of graduate students in statistics have challenged her exact ratio at three positive emotions for every one negative emotion as the "tipping point," but that argument misses the point.[1] On the whole, we thrive when we experience more positive than negative emotions. The evidence is still fairly clear that higher ratios of positive to negative emotions indicate higher levels of flourishing and resilience. And we also *need* negative emotions to navigate the world successfully.

When I first began learning about the science of positive psychology, I immediately gravitated to practicing gratitude. Each day, upon returning from work, I would pause to reflect on my day and identify a couple of things that went well. This was an effective way for me to transition from work mode to being a dad. The problem (or so I thought) was that "bad things" kept happening and my ability to react to them didn't necessarily improve. In one way, I could say that all that I was learning about happiness was actually making me less happy.

My reflection on this period of my life leads me to a couple of conclusions. First, my expectations were out of order. The simple practice of one exercise (even if it is done religiously) may not have the impact that I expected. The second realization was that negative emotions were not necessarily bad for me. In excess, they can contribute to poor outcomes at work, at home, and within our bodies, but in the moment, our emotions are simply telling us how we are interpreting the situation. So I took Fredrickson's quote ("Positive emotions are the seeds of resilience") and started to wield positivity as a tool.

Positivity Research

According to the research, a steady diet of positive emotions can contribute to living a more resilient life. Dozens of studies have been conducted that show the power of positivity.[2] The following is a sampling of some of my favorite findings.

- People report feeling less rushed and starved for time when they experience awe. Awe "involves perceptual vastness"[3] where we encounter something that is larger than us.
- We habituate to positive emotions. Our emotions respond more readily to new stimuli. Something that made you experience extreme joy is not going to have the same effect if you call upon these stimuli too often.
- Compassion can be learned. Yes, some people probably have an advantage in that they grew up in a very nurturing environment or there is a genetic tilt in this direction for them. Practicing a loving kindness meditation helped participants in one study show more compassion.
- Experiencing more positivity may make your immune system stronger. Some studies have shown a drop in interleukin and cortisol levels when positive emotions were introduced.
- High levels of stress and flow of cortisol can actually shrink the hippocampus. This leads to less perspective-taking which, in turn, could lead to lower ability to solve problems and generate options for creative solutions.

Fredrickson developed an interesting model about positive emotions and named it the Broaden and Build Theory. She did this to explain the mechanics of how positivity can help us and how it evolved. Fredrickson writes that "positive emotions increase the number of potential behavioral options." This is the "broaden" part of the theory. Positivity expands our range of possibilities. While intense negative emotions prepare us for survival in the moment, Fredrickson argues that positive emotions may lend themselves to preparing us for the long haul. The "build" part of the theory says that positivity can help us physically (better sleep and improved immune system functioning), socially (improved support and relationships), intellectually (greater creativity), and psychologically (higher resilience, more optimism).[4]

This is probably why the Gracie family has a saying of "Keep it playful" in their jiu-jitsu schools. Marco Moreno never gets too serious when teaching a new move. Rarely does an adult class go by without someone making a joke and everyone laughing. Each kids' class ends with a game of "run for your lives" in which Marco and his team of helpers kick a large, soft, inflatable ball at the kids while they run around on the mats. Once you're hit, you're out. The kids scream and laugh. The parents seem to enjoy this more than the kids. Students learn when they feel safe and experience humor.

Positive emotions elevate us to a higher place. They can make a bad day suddenly feel good. They can take a pessimistic view of our current situation and offer us hope. Many times, positive emotions are fuel for action. While negative emotions evolved to protect us in the moment and ensure that our genes will survive to the next generation, positive emotions help us build a better tomorrow. They help us build universities. They put men on the moon and they are helping us find solutions to other complex problems.

In one major study led by Teresa Amabile of the Harvard Business School, participants wrote about their days in online journals. These journals were independently and anonymously coded for emotions (joy, love, anger, fear, and sadness) by researchers. Another set of researchers used both the journals and independent ratings of the participants' work for creativity. The findings suggested that a general positive mood and the specific positive emotions of joy and love were predictors of creativity the same day that the emotions occurred. The occurrence of negative emotions predicted lower levels of creativity.[5]

This gets more interesting with another discovery in this same study. It turns out that positive emotions create momentum. Positivity was able to predict higher levels of creativity one day and two days later.[6] This seems to confirm the Broaden and Build Theory proposed by Fredrickson. And it makes a case for being aware of the emotional status of your family, your team, and your organization. Each of these groups is challenged with obstacles and issues each day. A small dose of positivity just might be the thing to help improve your problem-solving ability.

Additional research points to positivity being an asset that companies can access and a tool at their disposal.[7] Experiencing positive emotions, having a favorable view of the organization, and being intrinsically motivated by the work all lead to higher performance. Employees that experience more positive emotions get higher evaluations and bigger pay raises too. As we will see in the next section, negative emotions play a positive role at work and at home. Ignoring the constructive role of positive emotions cannot be ignored. In short, they don't just feel good, they are a resource for us to use to be more productive and reach our goals.

To gain more clarity on these emotions and why they evolved, Ed Diener and his colleagues conducted a literature review to learn more. Although it may be a surprise to some, it turns out that the research shows that most people are in a generally good mood, most of the time. In the absence of negative events, people tend to experience mild positive affect. Diener and his team refer to this as the "positive mood offset." And they theorize that positivity must have some evolutionary benefits. They argue that it must lead to some advantage that made reproduction more likely. Their review of the scientific literature shows that positive emotions can predict outcomes "such as creativity, planning, mating, and sociality." The researchers see it as an evolutionary advantage to experience higher levels of positivity.[8]

Joe Valerio played offensive line in the National Football League for five years after earning All-American status at the University of Pennsylvania, but he almost quit football at the age of 13. He was playing rec league football for his hometown of Ridley, Pennsylvania, and he was a little discouraged about the amount of playing time that he was receiving. He even started to think that he wasn't that good. All of this led to him thinking that he would leave the team or not sign up the next season when he would enter Ridley High School. This went on for a couple of weeks. Joe continued to go to practice and put in his time.

One day at the end of practice, Joe started to walk off the field and his coach put his arm around him and offered a couple simple words of encouragement. "Joe," the coach said, "please don't be discouraged with your playing time. Your teammates have all been playing longer than you, which is an advantage for them. But mark my words, you are going to be one helluva football player some day. Don't quit. Don't give up. Keep working hard."

At that moment, Joe experienced a cocktail of positive emotions that fueled his motivation for years. He felt hope for the first time that season that everything would work out. He felt inspired that someone was actually paying attention and saw something in him. He felt pride in his abilities as a football player after months of hard work. And he probably felt the affection of a coach who cared deeply not just about winning, but about a 13-year-old boy who just needed a little bit of love.

Did Joe feel hope, pride, inspiration, and love for another 12 years and the rest of his football career? Of course not; our emotions are fleeting. And there are some important differences between negative and positive affect to consider. Tiffany Ito and John Cacioppo conducted a study to learn more about the "positivity offset" and the "negativity bias." As mentioned earlier, the positivity offset is our tendency to experience positive emotions more frequently than negative emotions, particularly when there are neutral circumstances. The negativity bias, on the other hand, tells us that when we evaluate the situation in an undesirable fashion, the negative emotions that follow are more intense. They motivate us to act almost immediately. The researchers conclude that both of these are adaptive responses.

Hope and Motivation

We dedicated an entire chapter to optimism. We looked at it as if it were a skill. The benefits are many and, based on the research and my experience, I count it as a foundational skill for resilience. A close relative of optimism is the emotion of hope. Hope, in my opinion, has some foundational qualities, as well. The opposite, hopelessness, drains our motivation of acting at all. When we see a situation where there is no hope, we quit. Quitting can be an effective strategy at times. When it becomes our go-to strategy, it is an indicator of a lack of hope.

And hope is quite different from many other positive emotions in that it is usually born out of difficult circumstances. Think about Joe Valerio as a 13-year-old boy playing football; all the indicators predicted that football was not in the cards for him. Joe experienced hope walking off the field under the embrace of his coach. Hope gives a glimmer of light that we might be able to work the situation.

In a recent study with nearly 800 people from more than 40 countries, it was hope that emerged as the main factor that contributed to resilience.[9] Hope was able to help participants overcome negative life events. It allows you to open your mind to additional possibilities when considering how to confront a complex issue, which is also consistent with Fredrickson's Broaden and Build Theory. It seems to not only provide the spark to help us search for more routes to a particular destination, it may also be a source of motivation. I would like to see more research on hope, as it just may be the positive emotion that lasts long enough to keep us interested in attaining our goal.

Although all positive emotions may not be created equal, gratitude has received a lot of attention in the Positive Psychology community. Robert Emmons, a psychology professor at the University of California, Davis, has been studying gratitude for a number of years and is considered one of the world's leading experts on the subject. He defines this emotion first as "the acknowledgment of goodness in one's life." He writes that the second element of gratitude is "recognizing the source(s) of this goodness lie at least partially outside the self."[10] And there are multiple, research-backed benefits to practicing gratitude on a regular basis, all of which can contribute to our ability to effectively cope with and overcome adversity. Adults who regularly practice thankfulness report fewer symptoms of illness, have higher levels of satisfaction with life, and tend to be more optimistic about the future. In fact, practicing gratitude may not just be felt by the individual. In one study by Robert Emmons, after performing a thankfulness exercise, spouses of the participants rated the participants' subjective well-being as higher than before the exercise was conducted.[11] Want your significant other to see you in a more positive light? Be thankful.

Chang Liu, Director of Libraries in Loudoun County, Virginia, told me that she has been stressed about a number of things. She has a demanding career and is now facing the fact that her sons are out in the job market. As a loving mother, she wants to help and feels the burden of their search almost as much (if not more!) than them. At times, she feels overwhelmed with responsibility. How does she cope? Gratitude. She talks about how thankful she is for a rewarding career. She references the fact that she has two educated, kind, thoughtful, smart, and hardworking sons. She acknowledges her own health and vitality. And she can never forget her wonderful friends who are a great source of love and companionship. Gratitude is her weapon of choice when combating stress and anxiety.

She goes on to say that pausing and acknowledging the good in her life provides the spark that ignites her motivation to not just bounce back from difficulty, but bounce *forward* to pursue her goals. Chang says that these feelings of positivity help her "...feel centered and motivated to continue focusing on things that are within [her] control." Instead of ruminating on how bad things are Chang turns the table on adversity with a mindful pause that allows her to re-center and recognize the world is not ending. "There is much to be thankful for, so what can I do to get myself back on track?"

Too Much Stress and Anxiety

So we now know that healthy doses of positive emotions are good for us. They contribute to physical and psychological health. And they help us achieve our goals. But what happens when we don't get enough positivity? What happens when stress and anxiety are ever-present? One more question: Do you know why zebras don't get ulcers?

Robert Sapolsky, a professor and researcher at Stanford University, spent more than two decades in Africa studying one group of baboons to see how stress affected them.[12] Baboons experience stress at extremely high levels as they jockey for position within their group and engage in battles that take them within an inch of death. Zebras, as you can imagine, are at risk of death by attack from predators. It's a violent death that comes with little or no warning. The following points demonstrate a couple of interesting findings that have some bearing on our discussion.

- Continuous stress does not lead to illness. Continuous stress damages our immune system, which diminishes our ability to fight disease.
- It may be that higher levels of stress are a greater predictor of heart disease than "bad" cholesterol.
- Work outside the home is not necessarily a predictor of heart disease in women. However, their chances of developing heart disease increase if they do clerical work or have a boss that does not support them. (My theory on this is that women in these positions feel powerless and have lower levels of autonomy, which can lead to hopelessness.)

One of the major differences between us and other species in the animal kingdom is that we're really good at keeping things alive. Once a zebra has escaped the clutches of a cheetah, she goes back to eating grass, tending to her offspring and making more zebras. Humans are much more complex. We have the ability to ruminate about the past, project what may happen in the future, and make up stories for why things happened. We let things sit with us for days, weeks, months, and even years. Based on Sapolsky's research I think it is very safe to say that ruminating on a difficult situation is like giving ourselves a disease that just gets worse and worse over time.

Being sad doesn't feel good. Being anxious or feeling guilty isn't much fun, either. Each of these "negative" emotions serves a purpose, however. Sadness is an indication that our expectations have not been met or that we have experienced a loss. When we're anxious, something is telling us that the future is a little scary. We're being nudged to prepare for something to go wrong. Embarrassment evolved out of our need to connect with others to achieve more and survive so that our genes could be passed to the next generation. When we feel embarrassed, we feel the risk of losing our connection to a given group. If any of these uncomfortable feelings did not exist, we would be infinitely less effective.

There are a number of reasons why negative emotions are actually good for us. In several studies, researchers have discovered that people who are sad or depressed tend to be more accurate in assessing their situation. In one particular study, participants were first given an assessment to measure their level of depression. They were then led to a room in which they sat in front of a table that had a green light and a button next to it. Each participant was told that they could press the button or leave it alone. The participants did not know that the light went on and off at predetermined times. The button was not connected to the light in any way. When the session was over, participants were asked if they felt they had any control over the light. Those with higher levels of depression were accurate in stating that they had no control. The non-depressed participants, however, were more likely to overstate the amount of control they had over the light.[13]

What are the implications of this study? To start, if your situation requires you to be accurate, a touch of sadness and anxiety can help you be more successful. There is no need to make you or your team feel better. Also, don't hire all optimistic thinkers and those with upbeat personalities; you will not see risks until they become major issues.

A client of mine was the Chief Operating Officer (COO) of a company and he hired me to coach one of his executives to prepare her for the next level. The COO and my coachee didn't always see eye-to-eye, but they produced very positive results and had a very supportive relationship. One day, the COO saw me in his office and asked how the coaching was going. I told him we were making progress and that his executive was a quick learner and eager to improve. He then said, "You know what her biggest problem is? When she wakes up in the morning, she thinks about all the things that could go well that day. And she gets upset when things don't work out. I get up in the morning and think about all the things that could go wrong. And I am never disappointed."

My response focused on how this made them a great team. Instead of trying to sway each other to be more positive or negative, they would be better off appreciating each other's disposition and point of view. The two were an excellent team because of their differences, not in spite of them.

In one of the most famous psychological experiments, Walter Mischel set out to learn about delayed gratification. About 40 years ago, Mischel's team recruited a number of 4 year olds to participate. Individually, they were brought to a room with a member of the research team. On the table was a marshmallow (or some other treat chosen by the child). The researcher told each child that he or she would need to leave but would return shortly. Each child was told that they could have the treat if they wanted but they could have two of them if they waited until the researcher returned.

It turns out that the children who were able to delay their gratification and demonstrate self-control faired better in several domains of their lives in subsequent years. These children performed better academically and they were healthier and happier as well. They even made more money.[14]

We see this with Marilyn Frazier's life as well. Marilyn was divorced when her three children were very young. From the very beginning, she told the kids that being educated was the one sure path to being financially independent and secure. In Marilyn's house, you either earned good grades or there were consequences. She had an affinity for education and she saw it as a necessity for her kids. Marilyn also had the very strong desire to further her own education.

Shortly after her divorce, Marilyn got a job with the city of Massillon (in Ohio) as a secretary. (By the way, taking action is typical of resilient people. Marilyn was extremely worried about many aspects of her life after the divorce and she refused to sit and cry about it.) She did very well and received several promotions. At one point, she went back to school for a year but realized that the kids were not receiving the attention they needed. So she put off school again. Eventually, when the kids were older, Marilyn went back to school at night and on weekends to earn a bachelor's degree in sociology. By the end of her career, she was the housing administrator for the city. "The decision to put school off was not hard for me," Marilyn said, "I never had a problem putting my kids first." In short, Marilyn waited for the second marshmallow and the benefits were enormous: three very successful kids, a bachelor's degree, and an executive-level job in a very meaningful role that served her community.

Angela Duckworth is a MacArthur Fellowship award winner and a researcher at the University of Pennsylvania who has dedicated her career to the study of something she calls *grit*. She defines grit as "perseverance and passion for long-term goals." Duckworth and her team of researchers argue that the level of a person's grit is more important than their IQ. She has studied cadets at the United States Military Academy and National Spelling Bee participants to see what factors have the most impact on a person's success. In another study, grit was able to predict higher grade point averages and fewer job changes. Grit, it turns out, seems to win. And, it is unrelated to IQ.[15]

In one study, grit was negatively correlated to the number of hours that students watched television.[16] Self-discipline is not the only factor that leads to success, but it is necessary for grit. Those who earn success put off feeling good. They know that studying may not make them happy right now, or that putting a little extra effort into a report for management takes time away from leisure. They do this to gain the satisfaction of moving toward their goal and because they don't listen only to their emotions. Yes, enjoying an episode of *Seinfeld* feels good, but feeling good could just be the enemy to reaching goals and building even more self-efficacy. Rest and relaxation have their time and place. Pain can make us stronger as well.

How Loss Can Deliver Gain

Growing up in China in the 1970s and going off to a boarding school, Chang Liu says that "nothing was easy." The selection process to get into college was, in her words, "brutal." Only 4 percent of the population was afforded a college education. Chang's mother made one new dress for her each year. Her family of four people shared a one-room apartment. At boarding school, she shared a room with nine other girls. The food was terrible and she saw her family only after a 5-mile walk to the train station. School was in session for 10 hours a day and they studied until lights out.

It would not be fair to say that Chang's life is easy now. However, it would be fair to say that these experiences helped her be more resilient. Chang felt sadness from being away from her family. She experienced fatigue from the long days and anxiety when she contemplated what the future held. And she was lonely at times, even with nine girls in her dorm room. But she survived and successfully achieved her meaningful goal of attending Beijing University. In fact, she went on to earn a master's degree in library science. Difficult times are still stressful for Chang, but it was the challenging times in her past that made the future possible.

Gwen Farley's resilience, in part, comes from the devastating loss of her soul mate. Joe Valerio grew up in a household that experienced its fair share of turmoil and economic uncertainty. Jennifer, the mother of two disabled kids, is a more compassionate, patient person as a direct result of caring for them. Our schoolteacher, Jim, said, "I don't buy into this whole idea that easier is better. Difficulty and outright failure are not just natural by-products of the process of success–they are essential to growth and achievement."

Psychologist Daniel Kahneman earned a Nobel Prize in Economics in 2002 by proving that human beings did not always behave rationally and make objectively wise decisions. As a result, organizations are quick to hire him as a consultant. Knowing that teams fall into traps with too much positive thinking, Kahneman has his clients intentionally express negative thoughts to improve their chances of completing projects successfully.

A team is most vulnerable when it has decided on a direction. Often, no one speaks up about the risks for fear of being seen as being too negative. The team may have endured a long process with lots of disagreement, but they were able to make a decision. People are less apt to speak up with their concerns. At this very moment, Kahneman suggests injecting a little negativity. He calls it the "pre-mortem." Each member of the team is given several minutes to think about the team's decision. Specifically, they are instructed to fast forward one year and think about the decision as if everything with the project went wrong.

Kahneman writes that his clients (particularly those at the highest job titles) love this exercise. It gives the team *permission* to be negative.[17] So much of what teams do is influenced by personality, ambition, and other team dynamic emotions that we sometimes need to improve our decision-making.

A Little Sadness Is Good for Us

This is not an easy thing to hear when you are a teenager whose expectations were not met. Although my parents are two of the most supportive people in the world, my dad was quick to say, "Into each life a little rain must fall," to me when I started feeling sorry for myself. In high school, my world revolved around sports. So, not being named a starter on my basketball team or losing a game in football was devastating. My dad, a very successful civil engineer and executive, had his fair share of disappointment, but he didn't let it derail him. The value that he and my mom brought was to help me and my sisters understand that sadness and disappointment *now* does not mean sadness and disappointment *forever.* One of the great lessons of aging is that our emotions change through time. Experiencing deep sadness, regret, and anxiety help us learn and adapt to the environment.

When my sons and I leave my parents' home in New Jersey after staying for a couple of days, we're usually pretty quiet as we pull out of the driveway. We live more than four hours away and we don't get to see them as much as we would like. (In fact, I once asked if the boys wanted to go to the shore or to see their grandparents and they very quickly shouted, "Gams and Pop!") The last time we visited, I stopped at the end of the driveway and turned to my two quiet, sad-faced kids and said, "Can you imagine what our lives would be like if we weren't sad right now?" For the next couple of minutes, we talked about how much we loved Gams and Pop. We laughed about Pop getting food on his shirt and Gams saying, "Dowhatyouwant!" as if it were one word. The sadness, we all agreed, was an indicator that we loved Gams and Pop and that they loved us. Not a bad trade-off.

We have talked about the role of positive emotions when we face a setback. Positivity can provide that little nudge to create even the smallest movement that gets us moving toward a goal. But what if we were to super-size our positive emotions? What if we engaged in a constant stream of mega-positive emotions? Is there such a thing as too much positivity?

Gabriele Oettengen, a professor of psychology at New York University, was intrigued by the value of fantasizing as it related to goal attainment. As someone who had been following the research in positive psychology, she felt fairly confident that more positive thinking would mean reaching more goals. The basic idea she wanted to test was, for instance, if you visualize yourself getting the promotion or losing weight, you are more likely to actually do it.

According to several studies led by Oettengen, it turns out that fantasizing can actually make you *less* likely to achieve your goals.[18] When that something you fantasized about has occurred, your mind does not know the difference between you thinking that it happened and reality. So, your mind believes that the goal has been achieved. The feeling of positivity that occurs signals that you are safe and there is less need to act; your motivation to act *decreases*.

When it comes to simple tasks, fantasizing may help. When chasing after more difficult goals, however, what we find is that introducing some negative thinking brings motivation back up and prepares us for the inevitable: obstacles. Dreaming becomes an all-to-easy substitute for actually doing something.

Oettengen recommends something she refers to as "mental contrasting" when approaching an important goal that may be difficult to achieve. First, fantasize about the goal. This helps you decide if it is worth pursuing. Next, think about what *internal* obstacles may arise. Identify one or two thought patterns or behaviors that you might engage in that will get in the way. For instance, if your goal is weight loss and you are invited to a holiday party, imagine being tempted by the desserts in the room. Create an "if...then" statement that prepares you for this moment. It might sound like this, "*If* I walk into the room with all desserts, *then* I will immediately leave the room and think about how bad it would feel to let myself down." The key is that your contrasting involves something internal and something that you can control. And there is no need to come up with a list of possible obstacles. One will do. The point is to get your mind ready for obstacles in general. The person who has only fantasized skips this step and is blindsided by even the smallest impediment.[19]

All Emotions Have a Purpose

Now that you are armed with some positivity superpowers, please proceed with caution. When we start to master our ability to call upon the positive or negative affect that best suits our context, we cannot assume that those around us have the same knowledge. When we try to improve a negative person's mood by injecting some positivity it is almost a lock for backfiring. They may feel that you are not honoring their way of thinking. Autonomy is one of the most basic building blocks of motivation. And there is a certain level of autonomy that goes with our emotions. Maybe our most effective way of dealing with difficult situations is to be a little sad or angry for a short time. When that autonomy is not honored, we get pushback and probably even more negativity. When we don't force positivity on others, we are saying that we respect their feelings.

Instead, ask for permission to offer an alternative way to look at the situation. As discussed earlier, be careful of saying phrases such as "You should...", "You have to...", or "You need to..." This even goes for parents speaking with their children. If most of our sentences begin with this degree of certainty, be ready for some pushback. It might be more effective to ask, "Would you mind if I gave you some advice or just a different way to approach this?" and get a "no" versus not asking and getting an argument instead.

One thing we know for certain is that inhibiting our thoughts, beliefs, and emotions is damaging. According to the research of James Pennebaker, a psychologist at the University of Texas, holding in our emotions leads to higher levels of depression and a greater chance of physical ailments.

Pennebaker's research did not focus on positive *or* negative emotions. He and his team discovered that simply expressing any emotion was an effective tool for psychological health and resilience. Pennebaker also argues that the way we do it can impact our health as well. He advocates doing what he calls "emotionally expressive writing." Language helps us understand ourselves better and put trauma and adversity behind us. In multiple studies, people who wrote about their feelings (without inhibiting) for several nights in a row for just

15 to 20 minutes were less likely to see a doctor for physical ailments, had less depression, and achieved better grades.[20] In one study with a high-tech firm that laid off a large number of employees, those who followed Pennebaker's instructions on emotionally expressive writing were three times more likely to find a job within several months.[21]

Why did this happen? Those who wrote about the trauma of being laid off were able to put their anger and disappointment behind them so that they could focus on networking, updating their skills, looking for opportunities, or simply fixing their resumes. This is where Pennebaker's instructions differ from writing in a diary. With a diary, you continue to write and there is no end in sight. Writing for three to four nights in a row for 15 to 20 minutes at a time is like downloading our trauma on a thumb drive and getting it out of our heads.

Writing in this fashion helps us in several ways. First, it slows us down. When we talk to someone else or even think about adversity, our minds can "race." We're thinking, but there may not be too much mindfulness about accuracy, relevance, or exaggeration. We can gain new understandings by writing. It helps to create a level of objectivity. We write something and we read it as we're writing. We get to see the words and their meaning. We also get to learn more about ourselves. If we follow the instructions and just write without inhibiting beliefs and fears, hopes can be expressed. We can see patterns in our thinking that lead to greater self-awareness. Writing can also add structure where there was none previously. Those racing thoughts are put into organized sentences that allow us to see the situation more clearly.

Jennifer, our training professional in northern Virginia, has a mostly positive disposition, yet she sees the value and inevitability of experiencing negativity. Because she is so positive most of the time, others have begun to expect her upbeat friendliness all the time. "If I'm having a bad day, people are very quick to ask me if anything is wrong. Let's see, I just spent the night in the hospital with my son. Is it okay for me to be a little grumpy for one day?" Jennifer explains. Still, she opts for positivity because it works for her. She tries to distance herself from overly negative people but she refuses to push her positivity on others. As we were finishing our discussion on the role of positive emotions in her own life and resilience, she laughed and said, "I really try not to get too high or low. But when I'm down, I just turn on my favorite song. It's the spark that I need to turn things around and do something productive. You know it's really hard to be really mad or sad when you're singing."

It is foolish to disregard the power of negative emotions and how they benefit our ability to be resilient and live rich, meaningful lives. This is quite a shock to many who attend our resilience workshop. Some even debate that while maybe being sad, anxious, or embarrassed may be good for us, a feeling such as anger is just too damaging to ever be good for us. As I write these words, we are in the middle of one of the most interesting presidential campaigns in our nation's history. Of course, there are people on both sides of the aisle asking for less insults and for the end of the attack ads. I don't care for them, either, but they are never going away. They are simply too effective. Creating anger in your base of voters is more likely to spur action and get people out of their houses to vote. Negative emotions are powerful and will be a part of politics and being more effective as long as people inhabit this planet.

And remember that experiencing disappointment is actually good for us. As long as you do not turn that disappointment into an everlasting trauma, you will be stronger as a result. If you hold on to it, your trauma deepens and saps your resilience. The school teacher that I interviewed told me, "I resist this whole idea that easier is better." When we focus too much on feeling good, we diminish our ability to be effective. Don't obsess about how you feel right now. Know that your emotions are momentary and that each of them (positive or negative) can help you attain your goals.

The present paradox is: Living through adversity may be one of the best ways to strengthen your own resilience. It is *not* a guarantee that you will suffer in the future.

Finally, consider viewing positivity and negativity as a spectrum with extremes. One side is the overly negative world in which adversity turns into trauma. Anger is ever-present. Sadness is a loyal companion and anxiety diminishes our ability to take risks. This is a life of misery, inaction, and giving up. The other side is pure joy. It is filled with constant humor, awe, gratitude, and hope. In short, it is comfort. This world just does not exist. When the inevitable disappointment arrives, we are unprepared and ineffective. The most effective place to be is to harness your positivity and plant the seeds of resilience. Take risks and be prepared for setbacks. Use awe and inspiration to create movement toward goals but tap into your fear so that you are not completely surprised. Rick Hanson sums it up perfectly when he writes, "Taking in the good helps you see the good in yourself, in the world and others."[22] Our bias for negativity evolved to help our species survive, but it can damage our quality of life.

Take It or Leave It

- How often do you slow down to enjoy every bite of a home-cooked meal, every second that a loved one holds your hand, or the guitar solo in a song you have heard a thousand times? Think about a positive moment. Relive that moment by re-experiencing all the sensations of the moment: touch, smell, sound, and sight. Then, allow the positive emotions to wash all over you. Hold on to the joy, the love, the inspiration, or whatever positive emotion you felt for 10, 20, or even 30 seconds.
- Think about the places you visit, such as your favorite restaurant, your grocery store, or your child's school. Think about all the people who make that organization run by cleaning, stocking, and rearranging. If you get the chance, express your appreciation for their hard work. Make a habit of thanking custodians, bus drivers, and people that bus tables. Look for people who do the thankless jobs and express your gratitude.
- Take a five-minute walk outside. Savor the conditions, even if it is raining or there is a freezing wind.
- Who do you really admire? Mother Teresa? Martin Luther King? Mahatma Gandhi? Ronald Reagan? Eleanor Roosevelt? Create a heroes notebook. List the people you admire. Write about why you admire these people. What are their greatest accomplishments? What are their greatest strengths? Feel free to aspire to develop these strengths in yourself.
- Commit planned acts of kindness. Make it inconvenient for yourself. Take a day off from work or miss something important to you. Focus on doing something nice for others with no payment except the satisfaction of your good deed.
- How much do you sleep each night? Set a goal of getting at least eight hours of high-quality sleep every night. Most fitness trackers will do this for you automatically. Notice

how effective you are after a good night's sleep, after two good nights' sleep, and so on. Make sleep a priority in order to boost your mood and your ability to wield an emotion that helps you instead of being so tired that you react out of fatigue.

- Think about an important goal, project, or even a big meeting that is coming up. Spend a few moments visualizing the best outcome you can imagine. Savor the emotions of joy, pride, or whichever positive emotions you create. Next, consider what obstacle you may encounter within yourself. Finally, create an "if…then…" statement for your obstacle. It might read, "*If* my anger starts to rise, *then* I will take a break from the discussion." Don't be misled by the swell of positive emotions with important events and goals. Inject a little negativity to help you be more effective.
- Paying attention to your breath has long been a favorite of experts who look to help people with intense anxiety or anger in the moment. Be really curious about all the sensations that occur. How does the air feel on your lip as it travels to your nose? How does it feel traveling from your nostrils to your throat and into your lungs? Can you feel your shirt rise and fall as your chest expands? Make your inhale last for three to four seconds. More importantly, make your exhale seven to eight seconds. Every time you exhale, your parasympathetic nervous system kicks in and your heart rate slows. This, in turn, serves to reduce your blood pressure and move you closer toward feelings of peace and calm.

7

Building and Maintaining Supportive Relationships

We are Groot.

—Groot

"Say 'Joey is the best.' Come on, I want to hear you say 'Joey is the best,'" Tony would command his friends. Eventually, everyone would say "Joey is the best."

The Joey, in this case, is Joe Valerio. Tony is his older brother who used to bring him along to play basketball at a local park just outside of Philadelphia. In most cases, Joe was younger than everyone on the court by nine, 10, or 11 years, and his skills, of course, were way behind, too. Still, Tony would force the other players to include his little brother.

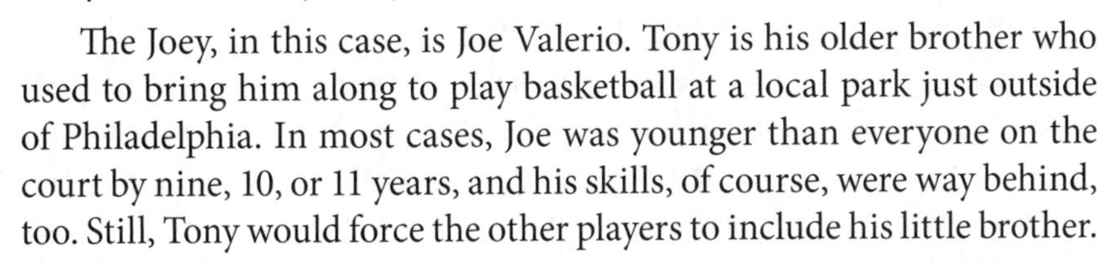

Tony believed in Joe so much that it started to rub off on the little kid who would grow to be 6-foot, 5-inches and weigh a muscular 300 pounds as an NFL lineman. But it wasn't always that way. Times were hard in the Valerio family. Illness and economic hardship seemed to be around every corner. Four fairly large boys shared one bedroom and two twin beds. (I've known Joe and his brother Tony for more than 25 years and I still can't make this picture work in my head!) His mother was in and out of the hospital and his father struggled with work.

When Joe talks about his early years, he immediately says, "I always felt love but things weren't always stable economically. I developed a lot of friendships. I surrounded myself with a lot of people who cared about me because I cared about them. When things are tough, I go back to what I'm good at; in the end it's relationships." Early on, Joe recognized that being successful at anything would require him to *invest* in supportive, intimate relationships.

For some people, relationships seem to come easy. I would argue that this is true and that people like Joe still engage in a great deal of effort to develop and maintain relationships. It's not a "sometime" thing. Joe and resilient people like him know that connection is at the heart of the human experience. And it is a foundational element of a resilient life.

The majority of this text has been devoted to how we live and experience the world as individuals. We've examined how to be more flexible. We've discussed the role of optimism as it relates to our resilience. We have touched on mindfulness, curiosity, and emotions. All of these are focused on our subjective, individual experiences. I stand by these areas as having an important role in our ability to learn from mistakes, bounce back from adversity, and achieve meaningful goals. The research is very clear, additionally, when it comes to close, supportive, intimate relationships. Connection offers us a number of benefits that are backed by more than 40 years of research.

Staying with the individual experience, for a moment, imagine that you stumble upon a bottle while you're at the beach. You pop the top off and out jumps a genie. This is a poor man's genie, unfortunately, and you only get one wish. And, you have to experience the results of your wish alone....

This (kind of) happened to me about 10 years ago. One of my clients asked me to deliver a team-building workshop in Orlando, Florida. We discussed the details that included the date, number of attendees, exact location, and the room setup. As I went about making my travel arrangements, it occurred to me that I would have a whole day to myself in Orlando and I was just minutes away from the happiest place on earth.

As I drove up to the Magic Kingdom, I felt like a little kid again. I parked my car, jumped on the tram, and then paid for my ticket. All the while, I was excited to get a needed break from work and do something that I enjoyed as a kid. As you may have guessed, within minutes my expectations were completely deflated. I went on a couple of rides only to find that I wanted to talk to someone about my experience. It was killing me not to have a friend or loved one to reminisce with. I could go on any ride I wanted. I could stop at any stand for whatever meal I wanted. But none of it seemed to really resonate without the ability to share it with another human being.

As it turns out, the research confirms my experience. Studies have shown that simply sharing your positive experiences with other people intensifies the emotions. Did you enjoy riding Thunder Mountain? Go tell your best friend. How did you feel when you earned that award at work? Call your parents and let them know. When we talk to someone else about our good experiences, we create a network of positive emotions that amplifies the signals between two or more people. Your discussion can be as simple as telling your significant other "this is nice" while you're watching TV together. It can be a little more intense as you tell the funny story about how you stumbled through your first kiss or when you hit your first home run in little league baseball.

The benefits go both ways, too. In one study led by Shelly Gable at the University of California, Los Angeles, researchers looked at how people responded to good news. To measure the responses as objectively as possible, they created two dichotomies. The first dimension measured whether the response was *de*structive or *con*structive. A destructive response belittled the good news by possibly pointing out how the good news wasn't as good as the other person stated. A constructive response focused on reliving the moment, enjoying the person's appreciation, and possibly offering a congratulatory reaction. The other dichotomy focused on the amount of effort that the person chose to exhibit as part of their response. A passive response may be only a few words while the responder is not fully present. An active response, on the other hand, is when the responder is present and fully invested in the moment.[1]

The Research

The research runs deeper when it comes to connection and relationships. One of my personal favorites points to the idea that we have greater problem-solving capabilities when we work with others. This may seem obvious, but there are forces in our culture that can nudge us to think that it is a sign of weakness to ask for help. It is impossible, of course, to know everything and be competent at everything. Striving for this is a recipe for a disappointing life. Being really good at strategic thinking may create a blind spot for details. Having an affinity for planning social gatherings could mean that you're not as good at thinking about what more introverted people desire. The bottom line is that obstacles, issues, and adversity are a lot less scary and much easier to manage when you have a trusted friend at your side.

When Joe Valerio started thinking about what to do after his football career, it was his wife who "forced" him to get an internship with a local TV station. She said that even making "$3.15 an hour will be worth it to put something besides football on your resume." Joe didn't pursue a career in journalism but he did get a sense of what life would be like after an NFL career. This little nudge would not have happened had it not been for his soul mate prodding him to beef up his resume. Today, Joe is a successful executive in the insurance industry thanks to his lovely wife.

A less apparent benefit of close-knit relationships is that they provide more meaning and purpose. We don't live in a vacuum. When you make significant connections to others, it's easier to see how hard work and managing through difficulty are easier to cope with when someone close to you is there. Truly supportive friends and family know how to empathize, when to simply listen, and when to encourage. Knowing that you are not completely alone in the universe is a powerful concept.

Chang talked about how difficult her early life was in China. *Every* comment about the difficulty was followed by a story about a teacher, a sibling, or a parent picking her up. Chang says that no matter how challenging her life was, she "always felt loved and supported." Living away from her parents at boarding school produced a fair amount of loneliness. But love was a constant companion. She had an English teacher that treated her like a granddaughter. When he worked with Chang, her confidence soared and he lit the spark of her intellectual curiosity that still burns to this day. On the weekends that she got to see her parents, her mother would make special meals that would keep with no refrigeration on a long train ride. Yes, the train rides back to school were sad, but Chang knew that although she was alone on the train, she was very much connected to people she loved.

According to Richard Davidson, being socially engaged holds other benefits, as well. When we connect with others, we are actually *less* likely to catch a cold, investing in relationships can lower your risk of coronary disease, and connected people get less infections and they seem to live longer on average. Relationships are good for us psychologically *and* physically.[2]

So, what are connection, support, and friendship? I argue that it is all love. Yes, the friendship that you have with your work colleague is love. The barista at Starbucks who remembers your "triple venti soy no foam latte" is just another friendly person on your way to work, right? No, it's love.

After toiling away identifying important benefits of positive emotions, Barbara Fredrickson took on the supreme emotion: love. Like many of us, her initial thoughts on the subject were pretty simple: meet someone in your 20s, fall in love, and develop that love for the next 70 years or so. She (and we) got it partly right. That is love, but using the scientific method and the latest technology, Fredrickson and her team of researchers discovered that love is made up of what she calls "micro moments" in which both people experience the connection. [3]

That's a pretty powerful way of thinking about love and connection. It can be difficult, at first, to think we experience love with the cashier at the grocery store, but that feeling of warmth you get when you recognize that he really does hope that you found everything is biological love at work.

Technology and Connection

If being connected to other people is so important why don't more people make this a priority? Why is the divorce rate so high? There are now more than one billion people on Facebook, many with hundreds of "friends," yet reports of people being lonely are on the rise. There are multiple forces at work. Among them is the role of smartphones, polarization, busy schedules, a focus on achievement, what we see in popular culture, and (once again) life is easier, on the whole.

Every day, I marvel at the power of my smartphone. The amount of information that is at my fingertips is absolutely amazing. In addition, if I desire, I can communicate with thousands of people on social media sites, email, SMS, video, or even make an old-fashioned voice call. The engineers of this era are developing new, impressive technologies every day that facilitate *interaction* between human beings. But we are losing our ability to *connect*. Sending a text message to someone on their birthday is not the same as dropping by to say hello. Clicking the "Like" button on Facebook is not the same as writing a handwritten letter to a friend praising him for his accomplishments.

Sherry Turkle, author of *Reclaiming Conversation: The Power of Talk in a Digital Age*, decided to put her research team to work to discover if all of this electronic communication was having an effect on our ability to engage in meaningful, fulfilling conversations. What we suspected since the first time we saw our children sitting on the couch with their friends not talking and their eyes focused on their phones has now been proven: *real* conversation is down and so is *real* connection.[4]

Turkle talks about the "three wishes" we have for our mobile devices: first, to always be heard; second, to put our attention elsewhere; and third, to never be alone.[5] Guess what's happening? We shout our thoughts into the Ethernet and the meaning is lost. When people do not see our body language, hear the pauses in our speech, or listen for the change in tone, they add their own meaning to what we have said. Consequently, no one hears us. And when we continually put our attention elsewhere (Facebook, email, and SMS), the person sitting right in front of us is no longer important. He or she almost ceases to exist, if even for a moment, and, she feels it. As for being alone, Turkle argues that learning to be alone means never really being lonely. The need to be surrounded by people (electronically or physically) means that it's harder to pause and listen to yourself.[6]

Consider some additional findings from Turkle on increased social media use.

- It leads to an increase in anxiety and symptoms of depression.
- It correlates with lower levels of empathy.
- It is harder to read other people's emotions.
- It leads to lower levels of self-awareness; people find it harder to name their own emotions.[7]

Consider this as well: Simply having a smartphone on the table when two people are talking inhibits conversation. We are less vulnerable. We share less. We are focused on what messages we might be missing. I share this information at the beginning of every workshop that I now facilitate. It's almost hard to look people in the eyes as they desperately want to keep their phone within eyesight, just in case....

And our gadgets make some things a little too easy. Have you ever been at a social gathering and someone asks a trivia question about an actor that was in a movie? What does everyone do almost immediately? They take out their phones and ask Google or Siri. Our desire to be right or first with the answer trumps our desire to engage in conversation. "Wrong" answers lead to more ideas. Conversation allows others to know how we think and what we know. This vulnerability creates more connections with human beings instead of "right" answers.

I make no secret about being a long-suffering Buffalo Bills fan. Ever since I saw those red, white, and blue uniforms with the charging buffalo on the helmet, I have been hooked (and disappointed!). Every Christmas, my mom tried to get me a Bills sweatshirt, a hat, or even a helmet. The problem was that in the 1970s there was no Internet and team merchandise was not nearly as prevalent as it is, today. Add on top of this that the Bills weren't very good and it made for a difficult task.

So my mom enlisted one of her best friends to drive around the state of New Jersey in search of anything that had the Bills logo on it. They used a paper map and their car to hit every sporting goods store within a 50-mile radius. During the car ride, they talked about their kids, their husbands, and anything else that came to their minds. Most stores didn't have what they wanted. They shared in the disappointment, walked back to the car, and tried again. In the meantime, they talked some more and became better friends. "Boy, that really brings back some memories," my mom said with a smile that spoke of things not being easy but still incredibly satisfying.

Speaking of the Buffalo Bills, I had the pleasure of interviewing Steve Tasker for this book. Steve was a ninth-round draft pick of the Houston Oilers in 1985. He spent two years with Houston before joining my beloved Bills in 1986, where at only 5-foot, 9-inches tall and 185 pounds (unbelievably small for the NFL, even back in the 1980s and 1990s) he made the Pro Bowl seven times as a special teams player.

I called Steve to talk about the Bills teams that went to four straight Super Bowls in the early 1990s...and lost all four times. I may not be objective but I think it's safe to say they may just be the most resilient team in NFL history. For four years, they bounced back after difficult losses in the nation's biggest sporting event and returned to the big game. How did they do it? These were high-priced athletes with mega-contracts who could have easily packed it in.

When I asked Steve about the Bills' resilience, he didn't talk about Xs and Os, strategies, or tactics. He talked about the cohesiveness of the team: "We had a great deal of camaraderie, including the entire coaching staff. We had a great sense of this being larger than just us as individuals or even just the players. I mean, I'm talking about the training staff, security guys, and secretaries, everyone was a part of it. Jim [Kelly] would have us over to the house after every home game. If you told him you couldn't make it because you had friends or family in town, he would just tell you to bring them! They became big extended family gatherings. We didn't just know wives and kids of the players like most teams. We knew friends and extended families; we were playing for something bigger than our team."

One of my fondest memories of being a kid was playing catch with my dad. I often joke with people that he deserves to be in the *Guinness Book of World Records* for never hesitating to get out of his chair when I would ask him to throw the ball. In fact, it got to the point that he didn't even say anything. If he was working on his computer or reading a book, he would simply close the laptop or put the book down and get up. The two of us would walk to the door, go outside, and throw the ball for as long as I wanted.

I got an occasional, "Thaaaaaat's it!" when I made a nice throw or some instructions on how to improve, but we didn't talk much. We didn't have to. My dad was there for me; there was no email, no text messages. I had him all to myself and I have never doubted for a second that my mom or dad would not move heaven and earth for me (and maybe even for my sisters!).

Today's world is overrun by practices, tutors, meetings, emails, and more. Another illusion of technology is that we can get it all done, but at what price? Many of the executives that I coach feel that they don't have time for one-on-one meetings with their direct reports to simply check in and provide coaching. Parents are scrambling to get kids to multiple activities, worried that their sixth graders don't have enough extracurricular accomplishments for their college applications.

Some of the most successful and resilient people I know make "stop doing" lists just for this reason. They know that their time is limited and that connections to loved ones really are more important than getting promoted or running a marathon. It's not to say that they don't have goals; they do, but they know how to flex when a loved one needs support. As a part of creating their "stop doing" lists, resilient people are also more likely to say no to additional activities and projects that take them away from their real priorities.

Connections at Work

Even the great (sometimes mean) Steve Jobs saw the value in having good people at work. Today, almost nothing is done in isolation. Teams, both permanent and temporary, come together to create work products. Individual effort and achievement is appreciated, but when someone is not seen as a "team player," it is usually not a good sign for his career.

According to the research of psychologists at the University of Michigan, it takes more than just a bunch of talented people to make an organization profitable. These psychologists theorize that "high-quality connections" make for a more effective team environment. When employees feel engaged, motivated, and safe, they are more productive.[8]

This is easier said than done. It turns out that there were three behaviors that the researchers witnessed on a consistent basis which led to these high-quality connections. The first behavior they refer to as "respectful engagement." It consists of being present with other people. When you are present, nothing else matters and the other person feels important. This leads to better listening and more curiosity. Respectful engagement is also being your authentic self. Adults can spot a phony a mile away. Without authenticity, trust is lower. Members of great teams acknowledge the contributions and circumstances of everyone on the team.

The second behavior identified by the research team was something they called "task enabling."[9] Today's shaky economic environment can sometimes lead to overly competitive behavior. The culture of the organization can motivate people to climb *over* each other in the best interests of the individual or work *with* each other in the best interests of the organization and all those in it. Great teams have employees who assist and coach each other. They're not looking for accolades or credit. They want to see the team achieve its goals. The managers of these teams are flexible in *how* the work gets done and work is shifted when some are overloaded.

The third behavior is my favorite: Great teams engage in "play."[10] They goof around a little. Practical jokes are not done at the expense of others. They bring people together. The games they play reduce stress and give team members a chance to view each other in a different context. This leads to learning and greater connection. Play makes us vulnerable. Being vulnerable increases trust.

Although trust is the third behavior listed by the researchers, it is number one in my opinion. And all too often, my coaching conversations center around interpersonal conflict where trust has eroded to dangerously low levels. Clients complain that a colleague cannot be trusted and speak as if they will never be able to trust the other person because of something they did two years ago. What I offer is the principle of reciprocity. When most human beings are given something, they attempt to reciprocate with some sort of payment. The Moonies, a religious cult that prospered in the 1970s, exploited this to raise millions of dollars, one flower at a time. They simply approached people in airports and other public places and handed weary travelers a daisy. Many people felt guilt for receiving something without payment so they forked over the first bit of currency they could find in their wallet or purse.

We don't like being indebted to each other. Unfortunately, groups like the Moonies and some sales organizations call this the "free sample to manipulate us." I offer being vulnerable as a way to show that you are ready to connect. Some of the most resilient and effective leaders that I work with are willing to share a personal story from their childhood or a revelation they made while going through a divorce. This vulnerability is usually met with sharing from the other person. And once again we get more connection and support.

Rener Gracie likes to call Jiu-Jitsu "the most effective martial art on the planet." As a student of his academy, I cannot disagree, as I have seen tremendous growth in my abilities in a relatively short timeframe. I have seen the same in my classmates. Rener attributes this, in part, to the fact that the Gracie Academy promotes safety and learning for all. Competition is a distant value with the Gracies.

Like life in general, Jiu-Jitsu training puts you in some very difficult, vulnerable positions in which one wrong move can lead to torn tendons, pulled muscles, and a whole lot of pain. When you "roll" with a friend or classmate, you put a lot of trust in that person. And the only way to achieve anything and get better is by working closely with other people. Rener said to me at the end of our conversation, "The only way forward is win-win."

Some years ago, I noticed a little icon that appeared on my LinkedIn profile that showed I had more than 500 connections on their site. It seemed like I was in some sort of elite status and I was encouraged to add more people to my network. I was proud, but then it dawned on me that there were truly only a few people on LinkedIn and Facebook that I would call close, supportive, intimate "friends."

The research is also pretty clear in this area. We can only sustain a handful of this type of relationship. It's not necessarily bad to have a lot of connections on LinkedIn or a thousand "friends" on Facebook.

But it creates the illusion of feeling loved when someone likes a photo of our kids and makes a comment about how cute they are in their Halloween costumes. True connection, we now know, requires in-person, face-to-face conversation with no distractions. It happens when we offer up a piece of ourselves and ask for help or just for someone to listen. It's more likely to happen when we're not so busy that we check interactions off of our to-do lists. It happens when we make it a priority.

When I have asked friends, family, and clients about what makes a great friend, one thing that comes up the most is that good friends seem to be nonjudgmental. This is pretty wishful thinking as I think we are all judging almost all of the time. It is almost an automatic process that has helped our species survive. Good friends know when to *suspend* their judgment. They do this with curiosity. True curiosity says that you are open and interested. It changes your behavior in that you start to ask questions which help the other person think differently about their situation. Curiosity also makes you a better listener. Instead of thinking of what you are going to say next, you crave new information that you can only get from listening.

The Value of Different Values

I recently read an email from a friend who was lamenting the disconnect between Republicans and Democrats. She wrote that she longed for the time when liberals and conservatives were friends who just disagreed on some things. Another friend recently posted something that was intended to discredit Donald Trump to her conservative friends. She said that Trump used to be friends with Hillary Clinton. I'm no fan of Trump or Clinton but can we really be disqualified by those with whom we choose to connect in different realms of our world?

Consider the research of Cass Sunstein, law professor at Harvard University. Sunstein authored a paper entitled "The Law of Group Polarization." In short, when people form an individual opinion on a subject and are then placed with others with a similar opinion, the group tends to adopt a more extreme position.[11]

Imagine a person who is asked her views on climate change and she states that she is skeptical of the so-called science behind this theory.

As part of a study in which she is asked to rate her skepticism on a scale of 1 to 10 (1: She is in complete agreement with the larger scientific community; 10: She feels that this is an elaborate hoax to further the interests of certain groups) and she selects 7. Next, she is placed in a room with others who are more skeptical and all of them rated their beliefs as a 7. The group is then asked by the moderator to discuss this issue for 30 minutes and come up with one number that represents the group's feelings on the issue. The group, after hearing from each member, turns in a 9 as their value.

This has been studied by a number of research teams; the consequences for our society and for our resilience are dangerous. We tend to buy homes in neighborhoods with people that share our politics. We go to dinner with people whose views agree with our own. Our Facebook friends are mostly on the same end of the spectrum as we are with regard to important issues. And we watch networks that support our views.

The danger is two-fold. First, we are not exposed to beliefs that are contrary to our own. And when they are brought up, they are drowned out by shouting, talking points on the side of the screen, and a waving American flag in the background. We start to see the world in black and white or good and bad when there is a great deal of gray and nuance. This also holds for the difficulties we face. When someone is rude to us at work, we seek a comforting voice to tell us how bad the other person is for what they did to us. Instead, the resilient person is okay with having her beliefs challenged by new evidence on climate change or gun control. The resilient person doesn't necessarily seek comfort after being embarrassed in a meeting, she asks for feedback on what she may have done to at least contribute to the situation.

The other danger in polarization is the anger that it creates. As Sunstein and other researchers have confirmed, we become more extreme in our views when we're with like-minded people.[12] Anger, as we discussed in the previous chapter, is not necessarily a bad thing. When it is expressed in its extreme and in groups (much like we saw at the 2016 Donald Trump political rallies) it clouds our ability to think rationally about complicated issues. Being resilient means, sometimes, being a little angry. When it clouds our judgment, however, we don't bounce back. We lash out.

Supportive relationships can be the backbone of resilient for individuals. As we've seen, being selective about whom we seek for support can make a difference, too. In the end, though, love can be the fuel that powers our resilience the most.

Daniel Porter, the Chief of Staff supporting the CEO of Europe for Asurion, was diagnosed with dystonia at the age of 12. It affects a person's ability to control the muscles. Most people with this disease get it in one of three areas of the body. It usually occurs in the legs, arms, or neck. Dan has it in all three areas. Playing sports was always a challenge and his speech pattern can be slurred and erratic. Dan was teased as a kid and denied jobs as an adult.

His family and close friends, however, provided Dan with the tough love and encouragement that makes him one of my heroes. He has not lost his faith in people. It's just the opposite. Dan turned his back on the people who rejected him because those who truly supported him..."instilled [him] with a deep belief that [he] had something to offer and contribute to society."

Take It or Leave It

- Try to avoid using the following phrases: "*You should,*" "*You need to,*" and "*You have.*" When your friends come to you for help be careful about immediately offering advice. Instead, focus on asking questions that help others help themselves. Your friends, family, and colleagues will appreciate your listening and not judging.
- Be on the lookout for other people bringing you good news. Practice being completely present. That means putting your phone out of site, closing your laptop, and stopping what you are doing. Engage this person's joy with questions, a smile, a hearty "congratulations," and maybe even a hug. Anything less than your full attention and sharing in this person's joy will turn him or her to someone else the next time good news comes their way.
- Create a board of advisors for your life. Look for people who are good listeners and who respect your values and are not trying to change you. Select people who see the world differently than you. Seek their counsel for big decisions and invest in time with them before you need them.
- Make a list of your core friends. This list will probably be 10 people or less. Ask each of them what they want or need from you. Give it to them.
- Make maintaining and building a network of friends a priority for you. Focus on meeting people who work in different industries. Look to connect with people who see the world differently than you do.
- Think about someone with whom you disagree. The next time you talk about the issue, consider changing your goal from winning, being right, or compelling the other person to do something (yes, even your kids…especially your kids!). Instead, try simply being curious about their stance. Try to learn more and talk less.

- Have you recently watched a good movie? Have you read a good book or watched a funny show? Share the experience with other people. The research shows that we can keep positive experiences alive by sharing them with others and even enhance the emotions you feel.
- Find a team and join it. Winning is much more fun when you do it with others. Losing is much more meaningful when experienced with others. And don't forget to enjoy the climb.
- Think of someone you don't necessarily trust as much as you would like right now. Ask him or her for help. It's a simple way to show some vulnerability and take the first step to repairing the relationship.
- Think about someone who helped you in your life but was not properly thanked. Write him or her a letter of thanks. Include what they did, how their effort may have been inconvenient, and how this help has had a major, positive impact on your life. Deliver the letter in person and read it. If you can't meet with this person, just write the letter anyway.
- Be super conscious of your phone when in the presence of others. Try putting it completely out of view when you're with other people. Pay attention to the people standing in front of you or sitting next to you.
- The next time you feel the urge to text a nice message to a friend, make a phone call instead. The next time you feel the urge to make a phone call to see how your friend is doing after a difficult day, go visit in person.
- Do something nice for someone else. Make it inconvenient for yourself by missing a day at work, your favorite show, or a couple of hours at the gym.
- Think about someone in your network who may be up against a difficult challenge. Make a handwritten note of encouragement.

- Pick a hobby that you can do with other people. My suggestion, of course, is to find a Gracie Jiu-Jitsu certified training center. Learn how to defend yourself, get a good workout, and make some friends.

8

Is It Time to Give Up?

It is not what we take up, but what we give up, that makes us rich.

—Henry Ward Beecher

My mom looked at me with love and a touch of warning and said, "Douglas, this is your last chance. Are you *absolutely* sure that you want to join the swim team this year?"

I looked up at her with the carefree attitude of a 9-year-old boy and replied, "Yeah."

"Okay," my mom said as she held a check while looking for any sign of hesitation. "Once I hand this check over, you're committed for the season."

This is how it went every October when my mom would sign me up for the winter season of AAU swimming. Every December, after the team had been practicing for about a month, I would tell my mom that I didn't like swimming anymore. I wanted to quit. My mom would tell me that I had committed to the team, she had paid money, and that quitting wasn't an option right now. I had to finish the season.

If I were to put myself in my parents' shoes, I probably would have handled this the same exact way. If you make a commitment to something that is only a couple of months long and you have to endure some hardship, you're sticking with it. There are exceptions, though, and quitting is a resilience tool that is available to all of us.

How We View Quitting

Our society does not look kindly on quitting. There are conscious and unconscious cues to warn us of the perils. Consider the following quotes and how powerful they are:

Winners never quit and quitters never win.
—Anonymous

Winning isn't everything. It's the only thing.
—Vince Lombardi

Failure is not an option.
—Gene Krantz

I'm pretty sure that several of my little league coaches shared the first quote with our teams. The dads meant well and tried to help us understand the value of perseverance and hard work. They wanted us to keep playing hard even when we were losing by 20 points with a minute to go.

There certainly is value in this concept but it's simply not accurate. All of the people interviewed for this book easily fit into the category of "winner." Each of them shared a story or two of how quitting one thing led to greater success. At the very minimum, quitting can be a learning experience.

The second quote was originally put forth by UCLA Bruins football coach Red Sanders. He said it in hopes of motivating a win on the gridiron. It was later brought to fame by Vince Lombardi who actually said, "Winning isn't everything. The will to win is the only thing." Lombardi was actually a little embarrassed about it. The man who went on to win five National Football League championships and have the Super Bowl trophy named after him was driven to win. But he valued the relationships, the hard work, and the process, as well.

Think about our economy. In one sense, it is only about winning the consumer's dollar. Wall Street is focused on quarterly results. Apple or Google could have one quarter in which they miss inflated expectations by one-tenth of a percentage and it becomes headline news... which sends their stock prices into a free fall. Eventually, this translates to employee evaluations based on accomplishments that are derived from a corporate scorecard. Effort is considered but results are what really count.

Finally, Gene Krantz uttered the famous words in the third quote during the Apollo 13 mission. When the NASA mission control team was at a breaking point and President Nixon wanted a statement about the mission, Krantz was sending a signal to his team and the astronauts who were thousands of miles away that absolutely nothing mattered but getting those three men home. Sleep, food, and families were less important than their new mission goal.

Krantz, the astronauts, and all those involved in returning the astronauts home are heroes and should be lauded for their incredible efforts. And in situations that are confronted by emergency room doctors, police officers, and firemen, saving a life is the *only* option. Krantz, like Lombardi and other coaches, inspired people to act heroically. As we will see, few of the situations we encounter are life and death. And the weight that we feel based on societal norms can feel overwhelming. Sometimes, quitting is the most resilient thing you can do.

Autonomy

Edward Deci is a psychology professor and researcher at the University of Rochester in New York State. He has focused on human motivation for the last four decades and his theory can be boiled down to three simple areas that he labels as "basic needs."[1] The first basic need of human beings is the "quest for autonomy." We desire the ability to choose the work we do, how we do it, when we do it, and any other elements that accompany a given task. Things that can get in the way of autonomy are deadlines, managers telling us exactly how to run a project, and parents who offer no choice to children, for instance.

The second basic need is "competence." People desire to reach a level of expertise in a given area. We strive for mastery, that is, to get better and better at activities that are important to us. Getting better and better at something provides a great deal of satisfaction. Deci argues that this is one example of how intrinsic motivation is what really drives performance. And once we offer extrinsic rewards (or punishments), we can almost never go back. In multiple studies, his team found that introducing rewards led to lower motivation. For instance, imagine that you enjoy painting but are not compensated for your efforts. Then, one day, someone says he will pay $500 for your latest piece of art, and all of a sudden it becomes incredibly difficult to disconnect something that was inherently pleasant from the reward. The task itself becomes less interesting and motivating.

Finally, Deci's third need is what he refers to as "relatedness." In short, human beings want to be loved and they want to love others. We desire to belong to a group. We find support and meaning when we are part of something bigger than ourselves. Being affiliated can also drive meaning and purpose.

Deci's work also suggests that autonomy trumps competency and relatedness. It is not that the latter are unimportant; it is that our desire for autonomy is that much stronger. We enter this world as curious beings attempting to direct the movie of our own lives. Deci writes, "Autonomy fuels growth and health because it allows people to experience themselves as themselves as the initiators or their own actions."[2]

So how does this relate to quitting? Deciding to discontinue a project, a job, or a relationship is a very personal decision. We are the lead actors in our lives and having someone else direct us takes away from the pleasure, the meaning, and the authenticity with which we live. Quitting, in some cases, reiterates our power to be the ultimate force in our lives.

Jennifer, our corporate training professional we met in earlier chapters, was married to an alcoholic. She did her best to help him, but the marriage ended in divorce and she took full custody of her two handicapped children. Several years later, she fell in love with another man. Unfortunately, he did not treat her very well. One day, the couple fell into another argument and Jennifer said to him, "You know, I'm really tired of your making me feel so bad."

His response may have been the one wise thing to ever come out of his mouth: "How can *I* make *you* feel anything? *You* choose how *you* feel! You're one of the strongest people I know. You're caring for two kids with very special needs and you put up with an abusive alcoholic for years, but that never seemed to get you down."

At first Jennifer thought her boyfriend wasn't taking responsibility for his actions. Upon further reflection, however, she realized he was right. She had the power to choose her reaction and what to do with her life. Soon after this conversation, Jennifer ended the relationship and struck out on her own again. Several years later, she met the man of her dreams and they have been married for more than 10 years. If Jennifer had not quit (twice!), I think it is safe to say her life would not be as rich as it is today.

We've all heard something like this before when we were striving toward an unattainable goal. The other person (a coach, a parent, a teacher) thought that their belief in you would create that motivation so you could achieve the impossible. And of course there are stories of great teachers, motivating coaches, and self-sacrificing parents who believed in students, players, and kids so much that great accomplishments followed. But deep down we knew we couldn't make it. It just wasn't possible.

The fact is we all have limits. Some goals are not achievable and not worth pursuing. Carsten Wrosch of Concordia University and a team of researchers examined the effects of chasing the impossible. How does it affect people when they continue to put effort into goals that cannot be achieved? It turns out that people in these cases have a lot more stress in their lives. They experience more negativity overall and they have higher levels of depressive symptoms. As for people who quit, Wrosch says that they "…have lower cortisol levels, and they have lower levels of systemic inflammation, which is a marker of immune functioning. And they develop fewer physical problems over time."[3] Quitting, it seems, can be good for your health.

Quitting is also *good* for reaching your goals…that is, your *other* goals. When you quit something that is impossible to realize or is making your life miserable, you free up resources for other goals that may be important to you. Leaving a job can give you the time and energy to write your book. Leaving a relationship that is doomed allows you to be alone and find yourself again. When the decision is ours, we own our lives.

Marilyn Frazier never found it easy to quit anything. She said, "Commitment and follow-through is very important to me. Giving up is not a part of who I am, therefore it was very difficult to give up on my marriage, even though it was not working. I learned that I could not accept nor change my husband. I could only control and change me and since I could not accept him, I had to end the marriage. I also learned that giving up and knowing when to walk away or quit are different." Marilyn was not only able to frame the decision properly, she owned it.

How to Fail Quickly (and Learn From It!)

What if we could take a magic pill that would help us evaluate our lives more objectively so that quitting would be easier to do under the "right" circumstances? Unfortunately, that pill does not exist, so we are better off thinking about failure in a completely different way.

To start, an entire portion of our economy has embraced the notion of failure as absolutely essential to its success. In fact, many of the business leaders in this area live by the motto of "fail quickly." It used to be that starting a business was an incredibly risky, expensive project. You had to build or rent a physical space. Within that space, you had to buy or lease lots of equipment. And, of course, it was usually necessary to hire a number of people.

Today, that model has flipped. You can start a business and run it out of your home without spending your life savings. Thanks to the technological advancements of the last 20 years, it's easier than ever. Still, to take your business to the next level usually requires additional capital. Venture capitalists and angel investors are much less likely to finance start-ups with tens of millions of dollars without proof that the business will have some success. Start-ups now plan to be "lean" for several years with a minimal number of employees, a couple of laptops, and a WordPress website. And they do little experiments with their product or service in which the goal is not necessarily profitable overnight. The goal is to learn as much as possible while spending as little as possible. Failure ceases to have a negative connotation as the team gains knowledge about their marketing, customers, and the product.

In the research of Carol Dweck, resilient people take on a growth mindset. What she has discovered throughout the last 30 years is being adopted by schools across America. In short, those with a growth mindset believe that their core abilities (intelligence, athletic ability, creativity, and so on) are developed through hard work and dedication.

On the other hand, those with a fixed mindset see those same abilities as simply immutable.[4]

The ramifications for one's resilience are important to consider. When a person with a fixed mindset fails, he sees this failure as a reflection of his abilities. It can be devastating since it signals to him and others that his limits are now on display. The person with a growth mindset is more likely to view failure like feedback from the system in which she lives. Failing a test for her starts a process of evaluation that moves her to evaluate her study habits, how she pays attention in class, and anything else that she can control to improve her grade. The fixed mindset individual labels himself as not smart enough and ceases to put forth more effort. He sees no point in this as his intelligence is fixed, according to his viewpoint.

One place in which accepting failure is critical is on the jiu-jitsu mats. When Rener Gracie talks about quitting, he says it's a "breakthrough and a trap" in our society. "There is a culture of never quitting in America," Rener told me, "In jiu-jitsu, when something is not working, we commit our energy to some other move that might give us a better chance of winning. That's not necessarily quitting; it's what I like to refer to as re-directing."

Famous Quitters

For all intents and purposes, I had the perfect childhood: two loving parents, excellent health, two (semi-interesting) sisters, and a nice place to grow up in Mahwah, New Jersey. My parents didn't spoil us with material goods and fancy vacations. Most of our meals were cooked by mom and hand-me-downs were a part of our wardrobes. When something didn't work out, it was not uncommon to hear my dad say, "This too shall pass."

It seems the quote was coined somewhere in the Middle East with the original author unknown and it can be applied to every major topic in this book. Seeing things as temporary can help us be more flexible in contemplating current difficulties. Seligman's research on the optimistic explanatory style also calls for something temporary. Being mindful and curious allows us to be objective and stresses that we live in the now. Emotions are temporary and issues that we have in our strongest relationships can stand the test of time.

The pain of quitting and failure is also temporary. If you know in your heart that moving on from a job, a project, or a relationship is the right thing to do but you're still afraid, that's okay. Shedding the expectations of a society, loved ones, and even ourselves can be agonizing. But the pain is temporary. Consider some of the following success stories and how quitting actually made success possible.

- After 13 years and 638 episodes personal finance guru Suze Orman quit her own show. She said it was a gut feeling and that if you stay with something for the wrong reasons (for example, money), someone else is going to make the decision for you.
- Charles Darwin quit a promising medical career when his heart wasn't into it. He ended up focusing on his passion of studying the world and his book *On the Origin of Species* changed the way we think about evolution.
- Steve Jobs quit college. He sat in on a calligraphy class that ignited his passion for beauty and form.
- Bill Gates dropped out of Harvard to form Microsoft. Not only did his software fuel a generation of businesses and students, he is now one of the greatest philanthropists on the planet.

In fifth grade, my teacher started a discussion about swimming. He talked about how he was a competitive swimmer and I guess someone told him that I was pretty good, so he asked me how the season was going. In front of 20 or so classmates I said, "I'm not swimming anymore. I quit." I don't think there were any audible gasps but it didn't feel good to say. I started playing basketball during the winter and it helped me make some of the best friends of my life. Almost every year, the guys from our CYO team pack up and head out for a "guys weekend" where we play golf, go fishing, and drink a beer or two. I didn't build a Fortune 500 company like Jobs or Gates. I didn't even play college basketball. I was really good at swimming but I'll take those friendships over everything. Quitting swimming was one of the best decisions I've ever made.

Take It or Leave It

If you're not sure about quitting, try some of these techniques to give you clarity and maybe even a little courage.

- Evaluate your situation and ask if the thing you would like to quit is negatively affecting other important areas of your life. How much better (or worse) will the rest of your life be if you quit?
- Are you living based on someone else's expectations? When you consider quitting, do you immediately think about how someone else will think if you follow through with it? If so, be aware that you may be living for someone else.
- What will you save by quitting? Time? Energy? Money? Will quitting allow you to focus the resources somewhere else that will add more value to your life?
- Consider Edward Deci's theory of motivation. Are any of them being compromised by *not* quitting? Do you need to re-assert your autonomy?
- Is your goal even remotely attainable? Remember that people who give up on these types of goals have less stress and anxiety in their lives.
- Run your situation by some trusted friends who are good at being objective. Don't tell them you are thinking about quitting. Ask them for some advice on what options you have in your situation. Make sure you get three to four options from each person. Discuss quitting as one of the options after they have exhausted their creativity. Talk through from different points of view.
- Adopt the growth mindset, as per Carol Dweck's research. Approach your life as one big opportunity to learn and improve.
- Take up a hobby where quitting is the norm. (Of course, jiu-jitsu is the first that comes to mind for me.)

- Remember that the pain of quitting is temporary. In fact, all emotions are temporary and "this too shall pass."
- Think about how you will feel about this decision in 10 days, 10 months, and 10 years. Try to create some objectivity and a little distance from your current strong emotions.
- Make a list of all the projects, situations, and people who drain you of your resilience. Find a way to avoid these things.
- Give yourself quitting goals. If you don't achieve success in a certain amount of time, you have given yourself permission to quit. For instance, if you have a start-up that is not generating as much revenue as you hoped, pick a revenue number that you would like to hit in six months. If you don't hit it, don't make excuses. Quit and move on to another opportunity.

Conclusion

Parting Thoughts

If you're going through hell, keep going.
—WINSTON CHURCHILL

Imagine a life with no stress, no anxiety, no sadness, no deadlines, and no adversity. All of your relationships are in great shape. Your health is absolutely perfect and money is not an issue. Sometimes I imagine winning the lottery or selling so many books that my financial future is completely secure. When life is a little tougher than usual, it's easy to drift off into this fantasy. Eventually, however, I realize that life is so much richer and more meaningful with the challenges that we face every day. Of course, it's nice to get a break every once in a while from difficulty. Winning and getting your way are the fruits of our hard labor.

Instead of comfort and ease, I urge you to imagine a life in which you are continuously tested; a life with ups *and* downs, victories and failures. Imagine a life in which you create and maintain close, supportive, intimate relationships and others help you bounce back and learn. Keep in mind that the only way to truly know if you are resilient is to be tested. And it's important to understand that you will be continuously tested. The good news is that you are already resilient. Of course I don't know you, but I do believe that everyone has the capacity to be resilient. The trick is to keep your sanity on the way to discovering this about yourself.

I used to visit my grandfather in the nursing home and he would say to me, "Douglas, I wish you all the luck in the world." It always made me feel good (and maybe that's why I feel so lucky). And for much of my life I have been focused on being successful financially, physically, emotionally, and any other way you can measure success. But please don't equate resilience with success. Some people are just plain lucky. Some are good and make their mark when luck presents itself. And, some sacrifice emotional and physical well-being for a life that measures success in dollars, cars, the size of a house, or even how many they count as friends, instead of being intimate with a few.

The basic point is that being "resilient" does not guarantee success in these other areas of your life. Being resilient does not bring a promise of financial success. It does not assure you that your relationships will be fruitful or that you will get the promotion at work that you have been striving toward for the last two years. Resilience can bring something greater: peace of mind that you have done your best and you can live your life according to your most deeply held values.

I have spoken with multiple, qualified psychologists about resilience and about how to measure it. Although there are assessments that probably do provide some interesting feedback, we are in agreement that no one has cracked the code on how to measure it yet. I chose to interview "resilient" people based on my subjective judgment of them. And so it is with you; you will know when you're being resilient and when you're not. You'll know when you're making progress and when you're regressing. Treat all of it like learning and you will be better off.

As we have seen in each of the five skills of resilience presented in this book, too much of a good thing can lead to poor results.

- **Flexibility.** There are times when our ability to see the situation from multiple points of view can paralyze us.
- **Optimism.** When we're overly optimistic, we fail to see the warning signs of impending risks and we end up unprepared and devastated.
- **Curiosity.** The thirst for information and knowledge can lead us away from doing, experimenting, and achieving. The human brain benefits from times when it is mindless.

- **Uplifting.** Too much positivity tells us that everything is okay and lowers our motivation to improve and strive for greater heights.
- **Support.** Never being alone and focusing on the number of friends can actually make us lonely and dependent. Too much attention on developing and maintaining relationships leaves no room for us as individuals.

But, what about resilience? Can you have too much of something that is so essential to survival and a meaningful life? I believe the answer is yes. Feeling the pain of life's ups and downs is uniquely human. Striving for perfection is unrealistic. It's dangerous and it robs us of opportunities to learn. We learn about our resilience. We gain tremendous amounts of confidence and build our self-efficacy when we overcome obstacles and act in resilient ways. Of course, we value the opinions of loved ones, bosses, coaches, and teachers. But the opinion that matters most is your own.

My group of resilient people see the space as well. I asked each of them the following question: If you were only able to give others just ONE piece of advice to be more resilient, what would it be?

Here is what they said:

- **Jennifer (corporate training professional):** "Don't hold on to the negative; let it go!"
- **Daniel Porter:** "Understand that struggle is the force nature exerts to create beauty and meaning. Resilience is the ability to embrace the forces railing against us to produce the meaning lying within us."
- **Joe Valerio:** "I feel resilience is best experienced when there is a known support group that you have confidence will be there for you in times of failure, trouble, and success. Therefore, ensure that you have built relationships with those who you can count on so you can try new things and experience lessons in failure knowing someone has your back."

- **Marilyn Frazier:** "I would have to say, remember, 'this too shall pass!' Difficult situations and circumstances may arise, but they don't have to define who we are. We should continue to plan and prepare for a better future in spite of such occurrences. As I have said before, prayer and meditation helped me remain focused on a positive future! Everyone has to find what works for them."
- **Chang Liu:** "Be relentlessly positive and surround yourself with people who bring joy to your life!"
- **Gwen Farley:** "Just keep moving forward."
- **Jim (elementary school teacher):** "My advice is about recognizing the need for resilience for the long haul and not just for the present. For previous generations, it seems that if you worked hard during your life then you would be granted a time in your life where you could relax and enjoy the fruits of your labors. I think this generation needs to think about the possibility that we are going to need to be more resilient than ever before and not just for the next 10 or 20 years. We need to be resilient for good, for the long haul."
- **Marco Moreno:** "Grand Master Rorion Gracie says: 'Self-defense is not just a set of techniques; it's a state of mind and it begins with the belief that you are worth defending.' Along these lines, I think to be more resilient the person has to start with the realization that he/she is worth fighting for."

Any book or person that promises you *the* one and only path to happiness, resilience, and success is selling you something that does not exist. I hope you made some notes in this book and that you find a way to incorporate some of the content to help you lead a more resilient life.

As I approached the end of the book, I paused to think about how it would end. What last piece of advice or concept could I share to get you on your way? I paused for a couple of days to distance myself from it and allow it to come to me when it was ready to reveal itself.

As my oldest son and I were leaving a very productive jiu-jitsu class, I remembered a saying that the students in our school like to share with each other. So, I asked my son, "Do you know what a black belt is in jiu-jitsu?"

Right on cue he answered, "A black belt is just a white belt who didn't give up."

As we have discussed, the right choice for you at a certain time might be quitting. The real thought behind the black belt saying is to keep showing up, keep breathing, keep swimming. You are already a black belt, it's just a matter of time until you see it in yourself.

Notes

Chapter 1

1. Martin Seligman. *Learned Optimism*. New York: A.A. Knopf, 1991.
2. Claudia Wallis. "The New Science of Happiness," *Time*, January, 2005.
3. *www.merriam-webster.com/dictionary/resilience*. Retrieved May 23, 2016.
4. Bill Murphy, Jr. "Want to Raise Resilient Kids? A Navy SEAL Says Always Do This," *Inc.*, June 6, 2016. *www.inc.com/bill-murphy-jr/10-things-mentally-tough-people-do-advice-from-a-former-navy-seal.html*
5. Karen Reivich and Andrew Shatté. *The Resilience Factor: 7 Essential Skills for Overcoming Life's Inevitable Obstacles*. New York: Broadway Books, 2002.
6. Brigid Schulte. *Overwhelmed–Work, Love, and Play When No One Has The Time.* New York: Sarah Crichton Books, 2014.
7. V.M. Gonzalez and G. Mark. "Constant, Constant, Multi-Tasking Craziness: Managing Multiple Working Spheres. April 25, 2004. Retrieved May 23, 2016. *http://dl.acm.org/citation.cfm?id=985707*
8. L. Christie. "Foreclosures up a record 81% in 2008." January 15, 2009. Retrieved May 23, 2016. *http://money.cnn.com/2009/01/15/real_estate/millions_in_foreclosure/*
9. Department of Psychology, Michigan State University. "Media multitasking is associated with symptoms of depression and social anxiety." November 5, 2012. Retrieved May 23, 2016. *www.ncbi.nlm.nih.gov/pubmed/23126438*

10. Eckhart Tolle. *The Power of Now: A Guide to Spiritual Enlightenment*. Novato, Calif.: New World Library, 1999.
11. S. Bradt. "Wandering Mind Not a Happy Mind." November 11, 2010. Retrieved May 23, 2016. *http://news.harvard.edu/gazette/story/2010/11/wandering-mind-not-a-happy-mind/*
12. Tolle, Eckhart. *The Power of Now: A Guide to Spiritual Enlightenment*. Novato, CA: New World Library, 1999.
13. "U.S. Smartphone Use in 2015." Pew Research Center, 2015. *www.pewinternet.org/2015/04/01/us-smartphone-use-in-2015/*
14. Todd B. Kashdan and Robert Biswas-Diener. *The Upside of Your Dark Side: Why Being Your Whole Self—not Just Your good Self—drives Success and Fulfillment*. Brilliance Audio, 2014.
15. R. Zilca. *Ride of Your Life: A Coast-to-Coast Guide to Finding* Inner Peace. Booktrope Editions, 2014.
16. Anne-Marie Slaughter. *Unfinished Business: Women, Men, Work, Family*. New York: Random House, 2015.
17. Barry Schwartz. *The Paradox of Choice: Why More Is Less*. New York: Ecco, 2004.
18. Daniel Porter. Personal email correspondence. December 12, 2015.
19. Brigid Schulte. *Overwhelmed–Work, Love, and Play When No One Has The Time*. New York: Sarah Crichton Books, 2014.

Chapter 2

1. Gabriele Oettingen. *Rethinking Positive Thinking: Inside the New Science of Motivation*. London: Current Publishing, 2014.
2. Angela Duckworth. *Grit: The Power of Passion and Perseverance*. New York: Scribner, 2016.
3. Tal Ben-Shahar. *The Pursuit of Perfect: How to Stop Chasing Perfection and Start Living a Richer, Happier Life*. New York: McGraw-Hill, 2009.
4. Sonja Lyubomirsky. *The How of Happiness: A Scientific Approach to Getting the Life You Want*. New York: Penguin Press, 2008.

Chapter 3

1. Chip Heath and Dan Heath. *Decisive: How to Make Better Choices in Life and Work*. New York: Crown Business, 2013.

Chapter 4

1. Martin Seligman. *Learned Optimism: How to Change Your Mind and Your Life*. New York: A.A. Knopf, 1991.
2. Barbara Ehrenreich. *Bright-sided: How the Relentless Promotion of Positive Thinking Has Undermined America*. New York: Metropolitan Books, 2009.
3. Martin Seligman. *Learned Optimism: How to Change Your Mind and Your Life*. New York: A.A. Knopf, 1991.
4. Daniel Porter. "Optimism and Mindfulness." E-mail message to author. February 10, 2016.
5. Rhonda Byrne.. *The Secret*. New York: Atria Books, 2006.
6. Martin Seligman. *Learned Optimism*. New York: A.A. Knopf, 1991.
7. Carol Dweck. *Mindset: The New Psychology of Success*. New York: Random House, 2006.
8. C.D. Ryff. "Happiness Is Everything, or Is It? Explorations on the Meaning of Psychological Well-Being." *Journal of Personality and Social Psychology*, 57, no. 6 (1989): 1069-1081. doi:10.1037/0022-3514.57.6.1069
9. Albert Bandura. "Self-efficacy: Toward a Unifying Theory of Behavioral Change." *Psychological Review* 84, no. 2 (1977): 191-215. doi:10.1037/0033-295x.84.2.191.
10. C. Peterson, W. Ruch, U. Beermann, N. Park, and M.E. Seligman. (2007). "Strengths of Character, Orientations to Happiness, and Life Satisfaction." *The Journal of Positive Psychology*, 2(3) (2007): 149-156. doi:10.1080/17439760701228938
11. R. Biswas-Diener, T.B. Kashdan, and G. Minhas. "A Dynamic Approach to Psychological Strength Development and Intervention." *The Journal of Positive Psychology*, 6 no. 2, (2011): 106-118. doi:10.1080/17439760.2010.545429
12. Marcus Buckingham and Donald O. Clifton. *Now, Discover Your Strengths*. New York: Free Press, 2001.
13. "OK Now What? Taking Action with Strength." December 20, 2013. Retrieved May 25, 2016. *www.viacharacter.org/resources/ok-now-what-taking-action-with-strength-by-ryan-m-niemiec-psy-d/*
14. A.M. Wood, P.A. Linley, J. Maltby, T.B. Kashdan, and R. Hurling, "Using Personal and Psychological Strengths Leads to Increases in Well-Being Over Time: A Longitudinal Study and the Development of the Strengths Use Questionnaire." *Personality*

and Individual Differences, 50 no. 1, (2011): 15-19. doi:10.1016/j.paid.2010.08.004

15. The People Behind the VIA Institute. Character Strengths, Positive Pschology Team: VIA Character. Accessed June 06, 2016. *www.viacharacter.org/www/About-Institute/The-People.*
16. Teresa Amabile and Steven Kramer. *The Progress Principle: Using Small Wins to Ignite Joy, Engagement, and Creativity at Work.* Boston, Mass.: Harvard Business Review Press, 2011.
17. Daniel Coyle. *The Talent Code: Greatness Isn't Born: It's Grown, Here's How.* New York: Bantam Books, 2009.
18. Ibid.
19. Michael Shermer. "As Luck Would Have It." *Scientific American.* Accessed June 06, 2016. *www.scientificamerican.com/article/as-luck-would-have-it/.*
20. Ibid.
21. Ibid.
22. Robert Biswas-Diener. *The Courage Quotient: How Science Can Make You Braver.* San Francisco, Calif.: Jossey-Bass, 2012.

Chapter 5

1. Todd B. Kashdan. *Curious?: Discover the Missing Ingredient to a Fulfilling Life.* New York: William Morrow, 2009.
2. Stay Mentally Active. Alzheimer's Association. Accessed June 06, 2016. *www.alz.org/we_can_help_stay_mentally_active.asp.*
3. The Search for Alzheimer's Prevention Strategies. September 2012. Retrieved May 25, 2016. *www.nia.nih.gov/alzheimers/publication/preventing-alzheimers-disease/search-alzheimers-prevention-strategies*
4. Carol S. Dweck. *Mindset: The New Psychology of Success.* New York: Random House, 2006.
5. K. Cherry, K. "Discover the History Behind IQ Tests." Retrieved May 25, 2016. *http://psychology.about.com/od/psychologicaltesting/a/int-history.htm*
6. Todd B. Kashdan. *Curious?: Discover the Missing Ingredient to a Fulfilling Life.* New York: William Morrow, 2009.
7. Liz Wiseman. *Rookie Smarts: Why Learning Beats Knowing in the New Game of Work.* New York: HarperBusiness, 2014.
8. Eline Snel. *Sitting Still like a Frog: Mindfulness Exercises for Kids (and Their Parents).* Boulder, Colo.: Shambhala, 2013.

9. Ibid
10. "A Wandering Mind Is an Unhappy Mind." *Science*. Accessed June 06, 2016. *http://science.sciencemag.org/content/330/6006/932.full?sid=3d27f229-6e05-4828-b560-1516e79f2a4d.*
11. Ibid.
12. Philip G. Zimbardo and John Boyd. *The Time Paradox: The New Psychology of Time That Will Change Your Life*. New York: Free Press, 2008.
13. Eckhart Tolle. *The Power of Now: A Guide to Spiritual Enlightenment*. Novato, Calif.: New World Library, 1999.
14. S. Achor. "Are the People Who Take Vacations the Ones Who Get Promoted?" June 12, 2015. Retrieved May 25, 2016. *https://hbr.org/2015/06/are-the-people-who-take-vacations-the-ones-who-get-promoted*
15. D. Moskovitz and J. Rosenstein. (2013, November 21). "Stop Obsessing About Productivity: Why Asana Embraces Mindfulness As A Business Model." Retrieved May 25, 2016. *www.fastcompany.com/3021943/bottom-line/stop-obsessing-about-productivity-why-asana-embraces-mindfulness-as-a-business-m*
16. A. Gorlick. (2009, August 24). "Media Multitaskers Pay Mental Price, Stanford Study Shows." Retrieved May 25, 2016. *http://news.stanford.edu/news/2009/august24/multitask-research-study-082409.html*
17. T. Brandberry. "Multitasking Damages Your Brain and Career, New Studies Suggest." October 8, 2015. Retrieved May 25, 2016. *www.forbes.com/sites/travisbradberry/2014/10/08/multitasking-damages-your-brain-and-career-new-studies-suggest/#2064b4df2c16*
18. P.L. Hill and N.A. Turiano. "Purpose in Life as a Predictor of Mortality Across Adulthood." *Psychological Science*, 25 vol. 7, (2014): 1482-1486. doi:10.1177/0956797614531799
19. K.C. Fox, S. Nijeboer, M.L. Dixon, J.L. Floman, M. Ellamil, S.P. Rumak, and K. Christoff. "Is Meditation Associated With Altered Brain Structure? A Systematic Review and Meta-Analysis of Morphometric Neuroimaging in Meditation Practitioners." *Neuroscience & Biobehavioral Reviews*, 43 (2014): 48-73. doi:10.1016/j.neubiorev.2014.03.016
20. Todd B. Kashdan and Robert Biswas-Diener. *The Upside of Your Dark Side: Why Being Your Whole Self—not Just Your good Self—drives Success and Fulfillment*. Brilliance Audio, 2014.

Chapter 6

1. B. Fredrickson. "The Value of Positive Emotions." *American Scientist*, 91 vol 4 (2003): 330. doi:10.1511/2003.4.330
2. B. Fredrickson. *Positivity*. New York: Crown Publishers, 2009.
3. M. Rudd, K.D. Vohs, and J. Aaker. "Awe Expands People's Perception of Time, Alters Decision Making, and Enhances Well-Being." *Psychological Science*, 23 vol. 10, (2003): 1130-1136.
4. PEP Lab. Retrieved May 25, 2016. *www.unc.edu/peplab/research.html*
5. B.M. Staw, R.I. Sutton, and L.H. Pelled. "Employee Positive Emotion and Favorable Outcomes at the Workplace." *Organization Science*, 5 vol. 1 (1994): 51-71. doi:10.1287/orsc.5.1.51
6. T. Ito and J. Cacioppo. "Variations on a Human Universal: Individual Differences in Positivity Offset and Negativity Bias." *Cognition & Emotion*, 19 vol. 1 (2005): 1-26. doi:10.1080/02699930441000120
7. Ed Diener, Ed and Robert Biswas-Diener. *Happiness: Unlocking the Mysteries of Psychological Wealth*. Malden, Mass.: Blackwell Pub., 2008.
8. E. Diener, S. Kanazawa, E.M. Suh, and S. Oishi. "Why People Are in a Generally Good Mood." *Personality and Social Psychology Review*. 19.3 (2014): 235-56.
9. Ibid.
10. Robert M. Sapolsky. *Why Zebras Don't Get Ulcers: A Guide to Stress, Stress-Related Diseases, and Coping*. New York: W.H. Freeman, 1994.
11. Todd B. Kashdan and Robert Biswas-Diener. *The Upside of Your Dark Side: Why Being Your Whole Self—not Just Your good Self—drives Success and Fulfillment*. Brilliance Audio, 2014.
12. Walter Mischel. *The Marshmallow Test: Mastering Self-Control*. New York: Little, Brown and Company, 2014.
13. A.L. Duckworth, C. Peterson, D.M. Matthews, and D.R. Kelly. "Grit: Perseverance and Passion for Long-Term Goals." *Journal of Personality and Social Psychology*, 92 vol. 6 1087-1101. doi:10.1037/0022-3514.92.6.1087
14. A.L. Duckworth and P.D. Quinn. (2009). "Development and Validation of the Short Grit Scale (Grit–S)." *Journal of Personality Assessment*, 91 vol. 2 (2009): 166-174. doi:10.1080/00223890802634290

15. Daniel Kahneman. *Thinking, Fast and Slow.* New York: Farrar, Straus, and Giroux, 2013.
16. G. Oettingen. "Rethinking Positive Thinking: Inside the New Science of Motivation." (2014)
17. Ibid.
18. J.W. Pennebaker. Opening up: The Healing Power of Confiding in Others. New York: The Guilford Press, 1997.
19. Ibid.
20. R. Hanson. "Hardwiring happiness: The New Brain Science of Contentment, Calm, and Confidence. Harmony, 2013.

Chapter 7

1. S.L. Gable, T.H. Reis, E.A. Impett, and E.R. Asher. "What Do You Do When Things Go Right? The Intrapersonal and Interpersonal Benefits of Sharing Positive Events." *Journal of Personality and Social Psychology*, 87 vol. 2 (2004): 228-245. doi:10.1037/0022-3514.87.2.228
2. R.J. Davidson and S. Begley. *The Emotional Life of Your Brain: How Its Unique Patterns Affect the Way You Think, Feel, and Live, and How You Can Change Them.* New York: Plume, 2013.
3. B. Fredrickson. *Love 2.0: Creating Happiness and Health in Moments of Connection.* New York: Plume, 2014.
4. S. Turkle. *Reclaiming Conversation: The Power of Talk in a Digital Age.* New York: Penguin Press , 2015.
5. Ibid.
6. Ibid.
7. Ibid.
8. J.P. Stephens, E. Heaphy, E., and J.E. Dutton. "High-quality Connections." *Oxford Handbooks Online.* 2011. doi:10.1093/oxfordhb/9780199734610.013.0029
9. Ibid.
10. Ibid.
11. C. Sunstein. "The Law of Group Polarization." *Debating Deliberative Democracy.* 80-101. doi:10.1002/9780470690734.ch4
12. Ibid.

Chapter 8

1. E.L. Deci and R. Flaste, R. *Why We Do What We Do: Understanding Self-Motivation.* New York: Penguins Books, 1996.
2. Ibid.
3. C. Wrosch, M.F. Scheier, G.E. Miller, R. Schulz, and C.S. Carver. "Adaptive Self-Regulation of Unattainable Goals: Goal Disengagement, Goal Reengagement, and Subjective Well-Being." *Personality and Social Psychology Bulletin*, 29 vol. 2 (2003): 1494-1508. doi:10.1177/0146167203256921
4. Carol S. Dweck. *Mindset: The New Psychology of Success.* New York: Random House, 2006.

Index

Acknowledgments

Finally, this book would not have been possible without the support, guidance, and love of a handful of people. My agent, Grace Freedson, was always available to help me with key decisions about the focus of the content and she believed in my book from day one. The world's best, best friend, Jim Hock, believed in me more than I believed in myself; he is the definition of a true friend. My fellow coaches have been so encouraging and three of them (Anne Loehr, Lori Zukin, and Brad Sterl) knew when to consult, when to coach, when to encourage, and when to be kindly critical. And my parents (Richard and Joyce Hensch) have encouraged me to be my best and do great things with a sense humility and modesty. All have taught me about the value of close, supportive relationships.